The Art of Music
Business Management

Mika Karhumaa

The Art of Music Business Management

FOR ARTISTS & MANAGERS

2nd Edition

Cover: Aleksi Manninen
Editor: Eloise Mikkonen
Layout: Tero Salmén
Chart implementations: Matti Mäkelä

© Mika Karhumaa 2024
ISBN 978-952-65029-2-2 (paperback)
ISBN 978-952-65029-1-5 (hardcover)
ISBN 978-952-65029-3-9 (PDF)
ISBN 978-952-65029-4-6 (EPUB)
See more: www.mikakarhumaa.fi
Mika Karhumaa uses a Lenovo computer.

CONTENTS

I. PROLOGUE

Hello my Friend! I hope you are doing well. For me, this is the last part of writing this book. The rest of the book is pretty much finalized and I can freely share my thoughts on it. I believe you have made the right choice in acquiring it and also I believe we share a common interest – the music business and especially management within it. It really doesn't matter in which role you are – or what the music business means to you. Of course, the book is primarily for artists and managers. Although the information included makes it useful for other music business professionals as well.

Prior to and whilst writing this book, I watched a lot of Netflix series – especially Spanish and Mexican ones. As a genre I hadn't previously been in touch with, I became attracted to the way the story is written. The plot, the characters, the elements and how all this is combined and presented.

Not revealing everything at once, but providing clear hints to what's happening next. The same happens in management and involves transitions – giving insights along the way as to why people are acting the way they are. The order of the presentation is of particular importance and even the smallest detail completely out of context, may be the most relevant reason for some intended outcome to happen. We are also interested in whether a goal can be achieved, for example when something doesn't work as hoped and how adjustment can make the journey come alive again.

I hope this structural decision makes this book not only understandable, but also insightful to read.

How does this relate to management and writing this book? Well, the modern music business isn't that different from screen writing. It includes a lot of similar ingredients, with reality providing hurdles – some of which turn out to be an opportunity and others just to distract you. Management is there to solve these situations.

In the modern music business, the perspective of the manager plays an even greater role. Management can be divided into three compartments. If these compartments are placed on a transparent wall in front of you, you have for yourself a navigator. Behind them loom the main areas of action – the four audiences of the music business. Those audiences are the stadium where everything happens. Imagine it as a baseball field. Whatever your current task is, place this 'structure' before your eyes and begin planning. This perspective also makes indirect effects more apparent.

Our greatest responsibility is to tell the story, but also to take note of the relevant grounding values, motives and goals for it. Also the business of it.

Even though I have tried to avoid unnecessary repetition, it may still have its place. Consider them the chorus of a song. A chorus is often repeated for a good reason. In the book, there are examples where something significant is consciously put at risk, like assignment of copyrights, for instance. In such cases, you should always proceed with caution. When navigating the more perilous aspects of management, it's essential to understand the stakes involved. That's why I revisit certain topics, even if they have already been discussed. For instance, when you trade your music publishing rights to achieve something significant elsewhere, there is always a cost. In this book, we explore how to manage these risks, and at times, this repetition is warranted.

Consider this book as a conversation and open to contemplation, as that's precisely what it aims to be. When discussing topics like artificial intelligence, the information in this book might be incomplete (or out of date). Therefore, don't take the concepts presented as arguments for or against, but rather try to see the bigger picture. It's about how its existence impacts management, where it's beneficial to leverage it, and where it's not.

I am using some words and concepts here that are fairly new and not necessarily well known by all. It's an assumption that some of you are more experienced than others. The years I've been managing artists, giving lectures on the subject or providing strategic support for those in need, I have noted one thing. There are a few essential preconditional setups that are always present in today's world, with online presence likely the most dominant. Therefore, I have put an emphasis on them whenever there's rational context. When dealing with a lot of details, it is just so easy to forget the original idea.

One thing to note is that even though this book discusses online presence extensively as our modern starting point, it is not the sole precondition; there are several others. The primary task of management is to facilitate an environment in which a particular task can be carried out. When it comes to artist management, these tasks are executed in sets. Preconditions are actions or tasks that need to be addressed before the implementation of a task. They can essentially be anything considered a prerequisite for success. If such an action is left undone, the entire project is likely to fail or otherwise fall short.

Furthermore, the journey is colored by various variables and indirect effects. Any factor along the way, even a minor change, may necessitate altering the entire approach. Especially at the beginning of a career when an artist is seeking breakthrough paths, the course may need adjustments multiple times.

In this second edition, there have been some significant improvements, especially to its structure. If you have read the first edition, you will notice this.

Without further ado, let's start this journey!

I would like to thank so many people. Many of you deserve thanks here, however I prefer to highlight the people who have contributed to the content of each book between publications. Although I would like to address all my supporters, one must draw the line. Therefore, if you cannot find your name here, it doesn't mean that I do not appreciate your contribution. It is very likely that you have been mentioned in my previous books.

Because family is the most important, I particularly want to thank them – not only for their endless patience. Even though the writing session itself doesn't necessarily consume much time – preparation for it may be present for years.

I would like to thank my lovely wife Oili Karhumaa, and Kerttu and Jermu Janhonen, our kids. I also want to thank my Mother, Terttu Karhumaa – she is one of my greatest supporters. My parents-in-law, Harri and Sisko – I am so lucky to have you. My Little Brother Pepe and his Family, they are quite many. The one that inspired me to start writing in the first place, My late Dad, Seppo. It was so easy to adjust oneself to writing with the examples you provided.

I would also like to thank Juhani Merimaa, Jorma Lillbacka, Annikki Lillbacka, Veli-Matti Lillbacka, Mandy Aubry, Anthony Churchman, Steve Mayall, Kushal Patel, Michelle Galas, Gianni Chiarparini, Maurizio Zandri, Fabio

Paluzzi, Tamar Hayduke, Giulia Torri, Dimitris Kazantzis, Heidi Holm, Helena Hautoniemi, Mari Pesonen, Veera Hjerppe, Maaria Toskala, Stuba Nikula, Mick Köppe, Maria Mannermaa, Katrine Friis Sønderby, Jenny Andreasson, Mac McIntosh, Jennifer Pyken, Rasmus Gustafsson, Karl Richter, Hannu Sormunen, Rikke Andersen, Josef Schartner, Hannes Tschurtz, Anna Turunen, Jenny Ring, Eric Campbell, Trygge Toven, Ryan Svendsen, Josef Schartner, Ian Smith, Mikko Merimaa, Iivari Nenonen, DJ Gunderson, Guenther Beer, Jens Deutscher, Laura Sparaco, Jennifer Porter, Dana Packard, Jone Nikula, Pekka Saarainen, Pekka Savolainen, Mikaela Savolainen, Jenni Kähkönen, Jack McConnell, Lacy Darryl Phillips, Erkka Oksanen, Sari Tiilikainen, Saija Vahe, Kristiina Lappalainen, Corina Avalos, Oliver Obolgogiani, Axel Thesleff, Prince Ayo Manuel Ajisebutu, Kamal Moo, Kristoph Jeffers, Louis Bo, Bhupendra Joshi, Matti Mäkelä, Timothy Williams, Sam Tall, Marilyn Reles-Lozano, Mikko Heino, Ditte Järvi, Aleksi Suomilammi, Joona Rinne, Elli Vihervaara, Ilias Kozas, Kati Ran, Fredrik Furu, Amanda Mäläskä, Emmi Malinen, Hanna-Maaria Tuomela, Saku Kallinen, Jutta Ruonansuu and Pasi Vapola.

A few names and institutions I would like to mention too.

Seinäjoki University of Applied Sciences and students who, through attending lectures, improved the content of this book. Of those numerous lectures, and through their preparation and interaction, it has been possible to build a whole new project that better takes into consideration modern information needs. Thanks specifically to Esa Leikkari and Jussi Kareinen for making these courses a possibility.

I would like thank Öli and Manchester Central Library, especially its Henry Watson Music Library. If I hadn't been invited to speak there, many refinements in this second edition might never have come into existence. I usually prefer longer sets, but this time, the essence had to be condensed. As a result, this modified approach brought a more precise perspective.

Two companies facilitate my activities. Hotel Bellevue, Pesaro, Italy and Turo, my wonderful clothing sponsor.

Our management team, Heidi Huttunen, Johanna Laakkonen, Susanne Ripsomaa, Viivi Koivu, Olli Jukkola, Petri Savola and Nicolas Roimola.

The artists I work with and have worked with – Winterborn, Melba Culp, Gentle Savage, IRENE, Chronoform, Delta Enigma, Rylos, AWA, Emmy June, Mustat Ruusut, Fredrik Furu, Hanna-Maaria Tuomela, Jennifer Porter and Annika Nord.

City of Kaarina, Finland – for providing all the services I need and kind atmosphere.

Last, but definitely not least – I would like to thank God for making all this possible.

2. INTRODUCTION

When we want to learn more about the characteristics of the music business – especially the modern version of it, management concepts provide fertile ground for delving into this. Even if many things have changed over the past decade, one thing remains the same. The music business is an artist-centered operational environment. No matter how much technology introduces new innovations and business opportunities, pretty much all of them are somehow related to the artists. That is, the artist's point of view is needed.

It's important not to be misled by technological advancements, even if, for example, artificial intelligence (AI) would be creating music in the future. There will always be a place for music created by humans; AI simply introduces a parallel and alternative way of working. For artist management, this is just one more added feature. In certain operations, it also presents a tremendous opportunity, which this book will later demonstrate.

It cannot be emphasized enough that management isn't necessarily a person, but a task. Not all artists are willing or capable of having a manager and if a manager is used, it is only for a specific task. Not available on a day-to-day basis. The ultimate responsibility of proper management belongs to the artist themselves. Taking on a manager is always a choice. That's why this book is titled The Art of Music Business Management – For Artists & Managers. Even though an artist wouldn't handle their own management, it is an advantage to understand what it all means. This way, one can better understand what they can do for their part. Similarly, various co-management solutions between the artist and manager are becoming increasingly common.

When an artist is aware of what modern management may consist of, they are better able to estimate their needs and whether it is reasonable to acquire it from industrial and/or other third-party arrangements. It is typical that this need varies at different stages of your career. Sometimes you need the external aid, although for some situations or tasks you can handle the situation better alone.

It is an assumption that, as a reader, you already have some kind of an understanding of what this book may contain. However, it doesn't matter if this would be your first step into the music business. The content has been explained in a way that it becomes clear. Reciprocally, if you already have the experience or a career in the field, this book may also be for you.

The sections pertaining to set up of an online presence, passive promotion, and the functions within the three compartments, along with their meaning, offer valuable information resources. Additionally, the part on digital standouts and its relevance across the four distinct audiences contributes to the wealth of information available.

If something within the book is unclear or confusing, Google or ask a friend. The music business is all about networking. You now have a great reason to reach out and approach someone you've been intending to. You will be surprised to know how much people inside this business are willing to help each other. Also, forget about titles and positions. The person you are talking with today might become a CEO tomorrow. Trust your own instincts. Something may also become clear with further reading.

The themes of this book are more about the overall concept of a subject rather than exact details. If something doesn't sit well with you, you should just skip it and move on. Sometimes it is more important to read between the lines.

For the same topic, there are multiple points of view and layers, making the music business complex. This requires management to be awake. Make your own evaluation.

There are a lot of details to know and continuously incoming – as technology develops or other business opportunities appear. It's important to not get lost in too many details. Each detail should have some connection to its origin, the story root and related business objective(s). If there are too many unattached elements, you cannot really control anything.

Read the following paragraphs carefully until you encounter the management compartment chart. Information related to the music business can conceptually be divided into technical and tactical components. Technical information manages details, while tactical information deals with managing operations and the operational perspective. We will revisit this division multiple times throughout the book. I will bring up this division whenever it is relevant.

For everything there is a time and a season and this also applies to learning the basics of music business management. You can always adapt some new feature and learn how to use it. These experiences are individual. New techniques or inventions can be momentary or permanent phenomena, management's most important job is to prioritize them.

Progression is the result of many factors. Sometimes an artist's story is more important and other times business. For management it is about use and acquisition of resources and this varies according to situation. The next four-part resource allocation sheds light on the matter. You can, in a simplified way, encounter four types of things. Things that already exist but progress does not require the contribution of others. Things that exist and progress requires others to contribute. Things that do not exist but progress does not require the contribution of others. Things that do not exist and success requires the involvement of others.

When looking at this perspective from a technical and tactical standpoint, we follow entirely different motivations. On the technical side, it's crucial to identify the type of situation. Am I in a situation where something exists, but its success depends on the cooperation of others? If so, we need to act accordingly. From the tactical perspective, we are interested in what route and solution will lead us to the desired outcome and what consequences it will have for the bigger picture.

The tactical aspect is often where management skills are tested – who can come up with a solution that works for that specific situation, the famous next logical step. On the other hand, even creativity has its limits; you need to know the boundaries before you start defining them. This is what makes technical information equally important.

The first structural observation is that management can be divided into three compartments. That is, the management functions in three compartments. This changes the view and allows us to focus on all the relevant business and related details, the technical side. When we switch back to the management point of view, it is the interdependent whole we are interested in, the tactical side. How do these things relate to each other and why.

Additionally, what's relevant for us as managers is understanding the extent to which we operate within different compartments and the scope of our mandate. If we're functioning in only one of them, our responsibilities should be confined to that one area, not extending beyond it. In modern management, it may not anymore necessarily be about all-round management on a day-to-day basis. Artists may have various different solutions for handling their affairs.

I have tried to keep a balance between technical and tactical issues. Sometimes there's more weight on the details when required. At other times, it's the tactical side that takes precedence. The book progresses from complex to more simple. This is one reason for occasional repetitions. They serve as landmarks that also help in progressing more smoothly. Remember, these are for references only – not to be strictly followed!

2.1. Control and Abandon

We will commence with the digital preconditions of this book and gradually transition to physical preconditions. Willem Dafoe has stated that it's all about control and abandon – and finding a balance between these two extremes. The same idea applies to artist management. At the very beginning, you must have some structure to get started. Each of us as a manager has our own unique approach. What you often aim for is control, to have your ducks in a row. However, there's a twist. As crucial as it is to attain control and the substantial amount of effort you put into it, you must be able to abandon it all in an instant if needed. It is just as important to realize that letting go may not be final. It's about finding a balance and being situationally aware.

When approaching these prerequisites from the perspective of the music business or artist management, it always entails three perspectives: that of the artist, the manager, and the current operation at hand. The million-dollar question in shaping, developing, and maintaining that structure is whose preferences take precedence, the artist's, the artist's narrative and goals, or the management's expertise. This is precisely the interface where one has to contemplate letting go regularly. The possibility is present every second. At times, we progress by leveraging management expertise, while at other times, it's the artist's narrative that resolves issues.

Another noteworthy aspect is embracing all three points of interest. It's often easy for a manager to forget themselves and focus solely on the artist and the operation. Rarely do we consider taking care of oneself as the primary responsibility in this role. If you can't take care of yourself, you won't be able to take care of others. Therefore, when we talk about letting go, it can also refer to this perspective. In addition to fostering an artist's online presence, remember that your own online presence also requires updates from time to time.

Conversely, when we speak of balance we do not infer that it is also a permanent state. It's about how to regulate the two extremes of control and abandon. In an ideal scenario, we possess the ability to read the situation so accurately that we know in each instance the proportion in which these factors should be present. Naturally, our goal is also to avoid being in the discomfort zone for extended periods and only when necessary.

An additional dimension to this equation arises when we consider the requirement of modern consistency. While we will delve into this topic in more detail later on, there is one related aspect we need to be aware of at this stage. Consistency can be assessed and achieved by utilizing the past, present, and future time frames.

The past is something that must always be taken into consideration – it paves the way for us. It also encompasses the brand message – if you want to put it that way. Everything that follows should be in line with what has already happened. If we deviate significantly from how we are accustomed to being seen, our four audiences may react differently than we desire. The present, in turn, is a spot where we can make a difference, here and now. All actions also align with this moment.

The future, on the other hand, is where we must embrace the past. When we take action in the present, it has consequences. When we make plans for the future, they have consequences too. When we talk about consistency now, we're not so much talking about consistency between things, but rather functional consistency – how different audiences evaluate our actions. In some situations, inconsistency between things is a perfectly logical outcome from a functional perspective.

Let's consider a marketing stunt executed by the management, in which the artist is introduced completely detached from their previous context. If, as a result of such an operation, the artist's popularity increases, attracting new audiences while maintaining the existing ones, it can be considered a success. Even though it may not fully align with the artist's previous image, what interests us now is its current actual impact. Will different audiences start seeing the artist differently and expect similar stunts, or can the artist revert to their previous image as if this had never happened?

Now it's crucial to look beyond the actions, to their invisible effects. If the artist's fans, the media, and the industry start perceiving things differently, it can easily be rectified by returning to the previous state. However, if algorithms start redefining the artist as a result of such an action, its consequences could be far-reaching, adverse, and difficult to correct. Consider that the popularity resulting from this deviation surpasses the artist's regular following; the artist may begin to be defined accordingly. Consequently, algorithms may prioritize mimicking this deviation over the artist's so-called normal style. When we discuss the functional side of a story, information, or any other content in the future, we mean this. Similarly, the essential question in that particular situation pertains to control. Are we ready to abandon everything from the past in pursuit of something 'better'? What are the consequences if we have a change of heart in the future and want to revert to the previous state?

Nowadays, differentiation often occurs in the digital realm, where it may not be immediately perceptible. Its results primarily reflect on algorithmic inputs. A skilled management can harness this in a way that aligns with the artist's image, goals, and narrative. We will revisit this topic later.

Therefore, as we continue with this book, let's keep this scenario in mind throughout.

Music Business Management

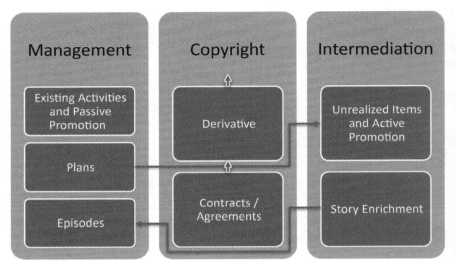

The above view is the first operating level that a manager should see. This view is always present, and if it could be drawn on a transparent wall, it is the starting point from which a manager begins their task. Before you start any task, you should take a stance on this. Determine which compartments you will operate on and under what conditions. Second, consider which compartments your work will have an impact. It is entirely possible that success in one compartment will reflect elsewhere. This matters for how your work should be rewarded and also for the actual responsibility you will have.

The music business management compartments consist of the management itself, contracts & copyright and related intermediation. These responsibilities are tasks of the manager, although the legal aspects, contracts & copyrights are usually completed by a lawyer.

In all-round management, where a manager operates in all three compartments on a day-to-day basis, the manager is also responsible for contracts and copyrights, even if they don't handle all the associated details themselves.

Therefore, it's not a bad idea to look for a suitable lawyer. If you already know in advance that you won't be handling these tasks, this is even more important. You can then work out with the artist how these responsibilities will be taken care of in the future. Taking action in good time, might allow you to receive a good offer regarding how your legal management will be handled, including the terms and price.

The agreement between the manager and the artist determines who is responsible for legal fees in different situations, as well as the manager's capacity. In the music business, there are managers with legal training.

Some contracts, due to their simplicity or repetitive nature may allow the manager to handle them without a lawyer. Nevertheless, each time you add a legal feature to your repertoire, it is highly recommended to gain experience first. If in two similar operations you have worked alongside a lawyer, you may already know what to do for the third. Some lawyers request copies of such transactions. This keeps them posted if something relevant is happening around the artist and also enables them to interfere if something goes wrong.

In an agreement this is usually placed under the 'Notices' section. The option 'with a courtesy copy to' the named lawyer, is informative and shows the professionalism involved.

Legal aid is always an added but necessary expense. You may have received a draft agreement not made by a lawyer although it appears so. The internet is full of templates for each and every potential situation. It may not exactly suit your situation and needs and even small deviations may turn out badly – especially when dealing with copyrights. As a rule, you should always use a lawyer who specializes in the music business, or at least the one who is familiar with contracts and copyright if there are any uncertainties. This should be emphasized before continuing any further.

With that being said, it is time to get to the point. The management itself, as a first compartment, could be described in many other ways. We could also talk about organization of things, maintenance & support or the professional guidance. It for sure is all of them. Still the management is a bespoke term in this context. This is mainly due to modern features of the music business. This same management is present when dealing with contracts & copyright, or the intermediation activity, the other two departments. It just have an adjusted objective. However, you can always take contracts and copyright out of this context and deal with them separately. You can also do the same for the interaction, take it as a single assignment. For the management itself, it isn't so. It requires or has at times required these other two compartments for its existence.

Management's first compartment relates to things that have already happened, or already exist. The goal is to embrace all that's essential and get rid of what doesn't belong. Believe me, removing unnecessary issues from your agenda can be a laborious task. These inessential items are often acquired along the path of reaching our goals. With experience, we learn how to avoid these.

The modern ideals of the music business embrace a self-initialized ignition and aspiration for economic and artistic freedom. Emphasis is no longer on intermediation in the way it used to be. Previously an artist needed a recording agreement to get started and this was the only goal for most artists and their management. Wider success was impossible without it. Some of this may still be true, but there's an alternative. Recording agreements are no longer the gatekeeper for getting your music heard globally. Business also doesn't take place behind closed doors anymore. You are free to release your music without the contribution of others and organize your activities the way you want and still have access to streaming platforms, radio play, sync placements and other meaningful plug-ins.

As a natural consequence of this, you now need to convince labels with completely different specifications. Traffic on your social media, exceeding a certain number of streams or some other economic or artistic prospect to get things started. Previously, negotiations could start easily at the very beginning – with only one hit-potential song, afterwhich the label arranged the rest.

Today requires careful evaluation at which stage you should make this approach. Too early, you may give the wrong impression, too late and the train may have already passed. No matter how impressive your production, you still need numbers to back you.

Fortunately, the industry isn't so black and white. An initial meeting with a label may not be successful in itself due to lacking numbers or unpreparedness. A second meeting showing huge progress however, may inspire them to engage with you. The same is true with all the other industrial arrangements.

Hence, no matter your destination, it is more important than ever to initially organize your own management. Only after this can one move on to the next activities. This first compartment is a kind of command center – where you decide what to do with the other two compartments. Management is associated with already existing activities, consequent to that, intermediation is about things not yet realized. The management/command center then evaluates feasibility of unrealized items and what to do next.

Management is also at the core of all kinds of manifestation. When we talk about modern management resembling screen writing, it happens right here. When management starts incorporating into the narrative, on top of and into existing material, things that have not yet materialized, it creates a framework.

The purpose of this information is to leak out into the awareness and process of all four audiences. It's kind of like casting a fishing lure. If nothing happens around the subject, it gradually fades away and ceases to exist. If such an action materializes into something, it's seen as a significant success, which in turn enhances the artist's online presence and value. Nowadays, it's quite common for this kind of scripting to be rehearsed for one audience while other audiences may not necessarily perceive it. We'll revisit this later.

Somewhere in between, above and below, in front and back, and on both sides are copyright & contracts. Even though management and related intermediation would be in a fully passive state, this third compartment is always active – if an artist has at least one publication or release and someone listens, royalties are due – regardless of what you are doing at that moment.

Copyright is effective everywhere, for the whole lifespan of a copyright piece. Because of this, copyright is also the most sacred protection area for an artist. We must use these assets wisely and for the big picture, copyright should be your pension and legacy. Whereas copyright is an asset, contracts are a tool. The more aware you are of different contract solutions, the better you can leverage copyrights as a means of negotiation.

Another thing to point out is copyright's metadata and power. The information connected to copyright and its credits are permanent in nature, which is why it has great search engine value. Once established, its content cannot be removed and thus each contribution establishes permanent credit.

Copyrights also serve a defining function, defining you through your productions. This has a significant impact on your online presence, as we will soon discover.

You could think of it as a tree, where each new production becomes a new branch and you as the trunk. Our task is not only to take care of those branches but also to ensure they stay securely attached to the trunk.

A well-organized management acts as a link between all these compartments. Management will monitor progress, make suggestions, take note on the artist's opinions and find ways to make things a reality.

One exclusion must be made. This book deals with the things relevant to the successful music business management. The things to pay attention when running related operations. We have deliberately excluded the music marketing outside the scope. We will tangent this topic yes, but only when it is necessary to the music business management. There are many reasons for that. The world is full of excellent books around the topic. It would be a waste of time to re-write these books. For example, Ari Herstand's How to Make it in the New Music Business is an excellent addition alongside to this book. More over, if you ever have an access to Music Ally's database, related Bulletin or any other material from them, you should take them immediately to your daily agenda. They are well updated with the information you need. The same is true with Music Business Worldwide.

When looking at music marketing from an artist management perspective, we are interested in how it can enhance a particular situation. Typically, a campaign is launched to achieve certain conditions that cannot be attained through other management means. It is then the management's task to regulate the impression so that it aligns with the artist's image, narrative and goals.

3. MANAGEMENT

3.1. Four Audiences

The next view, which is visible through those three compartments, is the audiences.

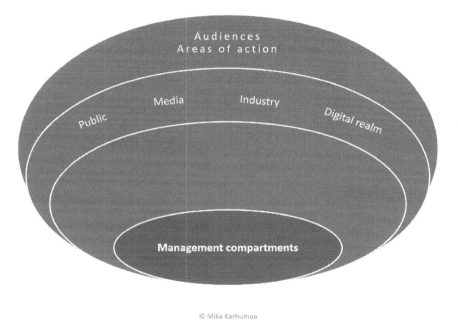

© Mika Karhumaa

There are four audiences and thereby four areas of action – depending completely on point of view. To better understand these, we need a few insights into these audiences. These audiences together and/or separately are the stadium where we deliver information about the artist, and also about yourself as a manager. How, why and what are the puzzle. It doesn't happen overnight, we need to build this puzzle piece by piece. This stadium is also the scene for this book. There are different seats available and it is now our job to learn to communicate with each of them, but also to prepare the artist to do the same.

These four audiences aren't the whole story. Among them are parallel realities, some of which you may call sub audiences. The metaverse is a phenomenon that deserves attention. You will likely need to think how to position yourself and your operations inside various metaverse communities in the future. These allow you to be present in wide-reaching forums – globally. Technology behind it evolves quickly and in turn enables more imaginative means to implement promotion. How we channel promotion within the four audience environments as well as the metaverse communities is strategically interesting. Some artists focus more on the metaverse, while others rely on traditional models. It's more common that promotion is a combination of both.

It is good to remember that trends continuously change. What's currently top notch, may lose its power in a few years. What makes a great manager is the ability to combine both old and new, merging promotion methods to best support the game plan and strategy.

3.1.1. Public and Media

Two audiences are the public and media – they are relatively easy to perceive. The line to the public should always be open and sacred. Fans have a reason to believe that you are honest with them.

Instead with media, it is a bit different. This is the space where ulterior motives can be acceptable. Everything that draws attention is content, it doesn't matter whether it is good or bad. Sometimes breaking boundaries results in outcomes not possible in another way.

Some choose also to color the story, but this requires discretion. The means and objective being sought are important here. The more acceptable the objective, the more leeway you have. Outright lying or intentional misleading is not accepted under any circumstances. One example would be to announce that your following has doubled in a year. If this has gone from 2000 followers and is now 4000, this is true. However, if this result is due to some paid promotion campaign, this is no longer straightforward. This is an outcome from the campaign, not necessarily the music. When using this kind of an achievement as a promotion argument, you should be really careful. A better option would be to just thank all of the people who have reacted and started following you. That's even a polite thing to do. The further an artificial claim of yours is from the truth, the more embarrassing it usually is.

At this point, it's essential to mention artificial intelligence and its capabilities. It's entirely possible that AI can uncover such tactics. It depends on how they are trained to operate in such situations. In any case, it's not favorable if your actions come under scrutiny simply because they appear suspicious.

On the other hand, these new followers may eventually become your fans and like your music. This can be newsworthy, no matter how it happened initially. Follower acquisition in this manner is completely acceptable, for some artists even advisable, but you should go public with this kind of achievement at the right moment.

Anyway, clarity is something we should strive for – to get things done through being straightforward. Equally important is to understand our audiences and try anticipate their reactions whenever possible.

If an artist's interview contains, say, one or two call-to-actions, either visible or hidden, they need to be easy to detect by the media and public. It's a matter of design how to include such teasers in the story at any given time. Consider an artist wanting to promote their upcoming tour. They can either say it directly or hide it in an obvious expression. Prior consideration is necessary if this information is intended for release in an interview.

Here as well, it's important to recognize the situation. Recall the four-part resource allocation; we are currently in a situation where something doesn't exist and its success depends on the cooperation of others. This is the purest intermediation scenario. From a management perspective, it's essential to align the action and its consequences so that it fits on top of and into what already exists.

A direct call-to-action may irritate the media. A journalist cannot always, or even necessarily want to act as an intermediary for advertisement or promotion. This may even be considered professionally offensive. If the interviewer has something else in mind, we should contemplate this and act accordingly. If our tour promotion doesn't fit that context, it should probably be forgotten. Otherwise we may jeopardize other great things. Nor do we want to endanger future collaboration with the media. Also, a reporter may not get money from their story. Therefore, it is not advisable to make things too difficult and set unnecessary conditions for its implementation. Know your audience in order to dictate how things can happen.

However, it isn't so black and white. There are always justified adjustments to try. When you present the same idea in a press kit or with prior contact and do it openly, the media's view may be more receptive. A subject may find its way into an interview even if not originally planned so. The process matters. If the interviewer is comfortable working with you, anything becomes possible. It depends how you approach people and can be a delicate thing. You get to know your audiences by spending time with them. Also, the more experience you gain, the better you learn to anticipate these reactions.

The same applies to the public. If you approach them, for example by means of social media, a call-to-action may lack the impact if there are no grounds for it. Otherwise it could be perceived as meaningless. With appropriate grounds a completely different reaction can occur. The content is the king. It doesn't necessarily request any outstanding marketing features, especially in the form of a call-to-action. It is more attractive when the introduction is comprehensive.

There's a reason for bringing up this call-to-action at the beginning of this book. It is commonly associated with paid promotions and can be for many different purposes. Acquiring more followers, more streams or to introduce new merchandise. Not all artists need call-to-actions, nor paid promotions. Because we are dealing with music business management, this should be highlighted. In many cases it can be a very useful tool when used correctly. It is essential to know however, that a call-to-action within paid promotion is different to a call-to-action within an artist's normal promotion. Paid promotion is a campaign or set of campaigns that have a premeditated timeline, however an artist's actual promotion runs daily – without any time limitation.

The nature of paid promotion is that it doesn't require contribution from others. The artist can dictate the terms. In an interview however, not much can be done without the interviewer.

The simplest way to describe paid promotion is that the target either takes the bate or not. They then decide how to react. Sometimes it leads to only one listen. A click may also be removed. On the other hand, it may result in a constant following, or some other outcome – the song may end up being put on personal playlists and you have another fan.

Paid promotions can be extremely useful for acquiring followers without expectations and without specific messages. But remember the results aren't the same as with organic following. You'll have to go the extra mile to get them truly engaged.

By understanding this difference, it is easier to understand how music business management and related promotion works. The context is completely different. Paid promotion achieves a premeditated effect; it is never a story. In actual promotion, the whole story is what's important. From a music business management compartment point of view, paid promotion can be organized through a hired promotional company – with management locating an appropriate company for the job.

These campaigns can be used in other ways too – for purposes not obvious. It may appear an artist is looking for additional followers, but the actual idea is to deliver an important message and not necessarily to gain followers. This can be useful if there is no other way to deliver a message.

That being said, it is essential to know that campaigns rarely leave a permanent mark on search engines without people's reactions enabling it. When people bring up topics in an ad or share the ad themselves, it may resonate on some level. Perhaps the most important thing to note at this point is that paid advertising itself doesn't increase social media capital and doesn't create a story-on-story effect. It lacks a point of contact and it disappears once a campaign is over. For this purpose, the artist needs to establish their own online presence. If this step is skipped, there is a risk that even campaigns with a significant budget will lack the impact they deserve. I will return to this issue later but this is valuable information to register for now. Remember the prologue about not revealing everything at once.

To conclude – this is a bidirectional street. In trying to gain visibility in the media and public, we also need their reactions to get the message through. It is strategically interesting at what can be achieved in follow-up measures and searches for people we try to approach. The most important thing is what they find and how well it correlates to the story we want to tell. Facilitation of such a mechanism is one of our greatest aims.

3.1.2. Industry

The remaining two audiences, industry itself and search engines, are not so simple. It is characteristic to have hidden agendas not visible to the public or media. When industry searches the same search terms, they monitor completely different things than the public. In general, industry is interested in an artist's stand-by and economic potential. This information is not always visible and requires prior information from the sector to be analyzed correctly, comparing artists' and managements' online presence as well as other business related variables against the industry's preferences itself.

Consider an artist being monitored by a label will also have their fan engagement and social media following assessed over time. If management is aware of this they can inform the industry through other means than email or one-on-one communication. An artist's social media often works even better and the results speak for themselves. This can explain elements that appear out of context – they are more than likely intended for the industry.

Management's task is to produce such content that industry is able to track and detect it – without specifically mentioning it. Success in this usually requires strategic construction of your network and expanding the sphere of influence with relevant hashtags or the like. A manager expands their operational reach throughout their career. Additionally, their industrial awareness improves along the way. The more the industry begins to recognize them, their methodologies and their expertise, the easier it becomes to communicate within the field. It's important to note that this work is ongoing and can be initiated immediately. It's not always a prerequisite to have an artist under management or approach people solely on behalf of that artist. Furthermore, the ultimate goal, to some extent, is reversed.

It's always ideal if the industry approaches you first, not the other way around. Then you know you've done something right.

3.1.3. Search Engines

The final audience is the search engines and everything that comes with it. This is probably the most important space in which to operate – strategically. It is worth pointing out that you alone are fully capable of affecting your online presence – without the contribution of others or the restrictions that others may impose. You only need to make your music available and let the related metadata handle the rest. It is also the foundation for your story – the production.

It's not wrong to say that before stepping onto the stage set by those four audiences, your online presence must be in order. This is the thing that sets modern music business apart from the past.

Today's music marketing can give back in many ways, providing multiple promotional possibilities and therefore earning opportunities – at least indirectly. This is great but requires some understanding of how they work. Constant activity and related engagement is often required on platforms to be topical. The more you post, the more traffic you acquire, but maintaining popularity based on this alone can be laborious – especially for artists. The most important question is how much time you are willing to invest, afterwhich you can decide how to go about it.

The most common myth about search engine activities are they do not directly provide economic results, however this isn't true. A well-maintained online presence is often a prerequisite for business and without it, you barely exist. It also enables relevant passive promotion. Many revenue streams in the music business are automated, as long as you've connected yourself correctly to pay sources. Once this is done, every online interaction related to you can lead to financially significant actions. This could increase your total streams, bring along sync placements, performances, or just generally – a new fan.

It's entirely possible that the priorities for promotion will reshape themselves with the advent of artificial intelligence. It's not out of the question that a strong and strategically developed passive promotion might, at least in part, overshadow active promotion. As more and more listeners utilize AI in their activities, they may like the control they have. This, in turn, could lead to active listening, rather than passive consumption of content generated by algorithms. AI is trained to search for artists that precisely match a certain criteria, rather than being influenced by ads and active promotion carried out by the music industry.

The kind of marketing that will emerge within AI in the future remains to be seen. Contemporary differentiation, as mentioned before, increasingly occurs in the digital realm rather than the physical. A well-curated artist presence may, in the future, prompt AI to promote the artist – only time will tell.

Search engines are often known for their best-known function, SEO, search engine optimization. However, from a music business management point of view, online presence optimization, OPO is more imperative. This is good to keep in mind. We are more interested in the content or left behind on the internet that people will find related to an artist than a preference over other artists.

It is easy to align promotion where needed or the most trendy. If TikTok has the best reach, acquire traffic there. If NFT's are the hottest thing, issue your own collectables or some other related items. Or consider another avenue, for instance in the metaverse – if it suits you, go there. This is all important and part of modern music business as long as you remember one thing. It is difficult to ride the wave without a foundation. Preconditions, like an online presence suitable for the purpose, must already be in place to allow smooth running of this. If you only take one thing from this book, I hope it's this.

You do not run search engine optimization (SEO) in competition with other artists or for other comparative purposes. You are creating an online presence to establish the most favorable content for those who search you. How this task is performed will affect how the other three audiences see you and your agenda. If you do not create anything for search engines to process, you may be defined by someone else. Take control of this possibility to be able to manage it.

3.1.4 Artificial Intelligence

Artificial intelligence (AI) is being widely discussed, for good reason. It is likely to change many things. Our focus lies in how it can impact management. In this book, I use scenarios that could be possible, but not necessarily definitive. Many things we've witnessed to date impact our experiences and also reshape our behaviors, the development of the business, and its focal points. It's such a vast innovation that it cannot be comprehensively addressed in this book. Therefore, please approach the concept and topic with some caution here.

In the context of artist management, we have the autonomy to decide how much to embrace technological advancements. Consequently, for some artists, technological progress is pervasive across all aspects of their operations, while for others, it appears only in 'essential' components. Whilst it's more often nowadays the job of management to determine this, it wouldn't be completely surprising if in the future, artists make their own determination regarding how, for instance, artificial intelligence aligns with their brand. For some artists, the fact that they consciously refrain from utilizing artificial intelligence is the factor that makes them popular. On the other hand, contemporary music could be entirely generated by artificial intelligence. As is often the case with new opportunities, the reality lies somewhere in between, encompassing both possibilities.

Another observation relates to terminology. We cannot anticipate all that artificial intelligence brings with it, and in the process of this book being published, many things have continued to evolve. Therefore, when discussing management, we can also refer to the digital realm, where everything takes place. When we address the natural operating environment, we have another useful point of view.

Additionally, instead of delving into discussions about how machine learning can create music and the implications for copyright, our focus lies in the strategic utilization of AI in artist management.

One important thing to note is that you yourself decide your relationship with artificial intelligence. The examples presented in this book encompass the normal contemplation and presentation of options, rather than direct recommendations you should follow.

Next, we will discuss the story root and its meaning with regards to online presence. While truthfulness is paramount when it comes to the story root, the associated narrative serves a slightly different purpose. It's crucial for artists to authenticate their story, especially their own version of it.

3.2. Story Root

First, a story root is a two-tier system consisting of the production and related story. The production, a composition or a recording is the necessary core. It is a physical fact, an embodiment. The related story is up to you and it's your job to decide how to authenticate it.

In today's management, the focus lies precisely in the process where authentication takes place. It is of great significance how it is executed and how different components are integrated into the whole. The term related story is connected to the metadata of the song and recording. It's like a product description where various relevant information about the song is provided.

In principle, the artist can decide what to include in their product description. Some artists keep it quite plain, while others find even the smallest details, values and other relevant information significant to include. From a music business perspective, the related story should at least contain accurate songwriter credits. Without this information, the artist cannot receive royalties, the song cannot be properly attributed to its creators, and management cannot earn their commission.

The most important moment is the release. At the time of release, content is decided, locked and can no longer be changed. Every time you make a release, it will add to the story root. It is up to you how large the story root will be.

Again, you can think of this as a tree. You are the trunk generating branches. Each branch represents a distinct production, either a composition or a recording. The more branches in your tree, the broader your production naturally is, and the greater your chances of success. However, economically, this is not always the case. It's possible for an artist to have only one strong branch in their tree, their biggest hit, while other branches remain in its shadow.

The related story includes important information about the song such as who has made it, the genre and the release date. In this book, 'related story' refers to the same concept and pertains to 'metadata' in general.

In addition to this, the artist may have the need to talk more about their production. The artist's personal version of events surrounding the production, such as the values behind it, may not necessarily be connected to the metadata, but could find its place in a different context. The artist may choose to delve into the background of a specific song, for example, in an interview, on their website, or a biography.

Now, with a story root and related story serving as the binding agent understood by search engines, it can connect these stories to that root. Every hit directed towards such a story root increases its value. And this, in turn, creates a story-on-story effect.

It entirely depends on the platform as to what type of information can be included and where. For instance, when you release music on Spotify, during the uploading phase, you can include a surprising amount of information about the release and all of it can have metadata value. That information then travels in a different way along with the story root from that point forward.

The permanent nature of this story root is a good reason to be careful how you want to identify your songs – and yourself in it. That is generated automatically at the time of publication. If you don't react with an appropriate related story at that moment, it might be difficult to rectify later. Google starts determining a publisher's attribute based on publication at the time of its release. You want to ensure that information is correct.

A small note before we proceed: the manager also has their own story root – it just takes a little longer to come alive. This is due to copyright issues and the fact that the management role is derivative. A manager needs an artist to become a manager. While an artist merely needs a release, a manager often needs to establish merit before search engines start interpreting them as a manager. However, sometimes merely signing a management contract can initiate this effect. In any case, the takeaway here is that each manager needs to consider how this *defining of becoming* a manager will be done in the future on their own terms.

The story root is an enabler – it's the artist's authentic view. When it's set up correctly, it can take the artist almost anywhere. It can introduce the artist to audiences the artist wouldn't normally reach. At this point, it's good to emphasize the passive dimension. The digital realm is constantly processing its environment. When a user's inquiries come close enough, this mechanism may offer the artist as an option – even in remote contexts. If this leads to contact or any other form of engagement, the artist's promotion can be considered successful in the passive dimension. That is, the artist didn't actively initiate this outcome, but it occurs retrospectively, supported by the online presence built by the artist.

To sum up, an artist's story always begins with their first release. It doesn't necessarily have to be a major breakthrough, but can simply be one publication. Everything that happens after that moment defines how the artist is perceived in this digital reality. It is the responsibility of the artist's management to shape the artist's online presence through their actions so that it aligns with goals and connects the artist's music to revenue sources.

Metadata establishes an irreversible link between the production and its creators, provided you have registered it correctly. Every release becomes an addition to your catalog. Hence, the minimum requirement for the story root is at least one publication or release. The more releases, the better base for these stories. Link your production to the story in a way that fits best. Be consistent here.

Whilst the information about music is permanent, the content associated with a story, a personal view, may change.

A love song may develop other meanings as the years go by. Many songs have lyrics allowing alternative interpretations.

Still, the information about the song remains the same. The production is always the core, not the story around it. The story around it provides additional information, but is optional. This provides an artist with opportunity, but doesn't have to be used.

The great thing about a song or recording's metadata is that it is somewhat neutral. If a piece of an artist's production, for example, acts as a binding agent for a social media post, it influences all participants in different ways.

Consider a scenario where a journalist who has interviewed the artist publishes their own post about the interview and what it means to them. The artist reciprocates with thanks and shares the journalist's post on their own social media. Both online presences address the same event, the article, from different perspectives and entirely different starting points – creating a story-on-story effect for that interview. If the interview is conducted in connection with the artist's newly released song and discusses that specific track, with immediate hits including the interview itself, the journalist's post and the artist's response, we now have three distinct versions, all tracing back to that artist's song – the story's root context. When this interview resonates with its readers and both posts resonate with their followers, we introduce indirect hits into the mix. All of these elements together contribute to a significant story-on-story effect, expanding the artist's promotion to broader audiences.

For an artist, this is a wonderful opportunity. In an ideal situation, a song or recording may even have a life of its own, potentially even departing from the artist's original idea.

Furthermore, it's highly likely that AI will become a more adept data handler than we're accustomed to. Production metadata serves purposes beyond describing it or the artist. On a song-by-song basis, it can contain crucial information about copyrights and ownership. For example, the metadata within a track may mention possible synchronization placements, where to obtain licenses for it, and how easy this is. Having rights available from the same source and potentially within 15 minutes provides a competitive advantage over others.

With regard to the story root, all these inclusions are relevant – no matter your opinion about the related story. Through each and every addition related to you and your production, search engines and algorithms begin to form an idea of you. This evaluation and related processing is a never-ending story.

Self-included classifications are particularly important. That is, the description included when uploading your music, for example, on Spotify. This information contains many identifiers for future use. As a result, search engines also make their own conclusions and classify you and your production. If you classify your song as rock music, Google will probably define you as a rock band at some point.

Production's inclusion itself is a technical operation. Search engines appreciate accurate results. Therefore, each and every uploading phase should be handled with care – rock music can accidentally be mislabeled as classical music. If anyone else is doing this operation for you, ensure it will be done correctly. Production is attributed to you in person. Once you receive this credit, it is forever. It is up to you what you will say about this contribution.

That was a few points about the related story. It is good to note that all four audiences will ultimately have their own understanding of everything. This creates a story-on-story effect.

3.3. Homepages

Rarely do we consider that a homepage may be much more than it appears on the surface. It's a place where the functional aspect of information can be most autonomously incorporated.

It refers to the significance of information regarding its function or relevance to something – how or what a certain presented subject matter pertains to or signifies. For instance, when an artist discusses their song, all related perspectives, reactions, opinions, and other elements always, to some extent, circle back to that particular track. The meaning of the song to the artist as its creator is entirely different from its meaning to a listener. The differences in these functions are one factor that creates such desired 'story-on-story' effects.

An artist's homepage is a space the artist can fully govern. From here, you can initiate and set the stage for many operations. Provide information about upcoming releases well before the release. This will provide Google time to process. If the artist succeeds they get their point of view out before others. It doesn't matter even if the new song doesn't exist as a story root yet. If you can specify it by name, it automatically gets linked up at its time of release. This may influence others. For example, prior to an interview, media often check what can be found about an artist online and may make an approach accordingly.

A website has been produced correctly when it serves the strategic purposes you have or want to define – not necessarily what is considered relevant against industrial or other external expectations. It's perfectly natural to emphasize business perspectives at different times and then go back to the original storyline, depending on your current objectives. Sometimes it makes sense to see how things flow themselves, other times it is worthwhile intervening.

This means there can be parallel motives simultaneously. It is up to the artist which should come first. It is never recommended to cause confusion until the robust online presence is established. When all audiences begin to understand your story and its related nuances correctly, then, and only then, you can start taking it easy.

Homepage content appears differently to each audience and participant, and this isn't always visible externally. The non-visible content only you and Google fully understand usually has an objective. Consider the way Google will process information to make keywords, affiliated links or other external associations work for you. These links can be external and internal. External links typically refer to external evidence of an event, experience or some production and your involvement in it. If you're visiting New York, you can link the location or other New York-related association in your text with a backlink or keyword. You decide how the New York-related snippet fits best into your story. Outwardly, such a note appears a harmless addition, showcasing only the immediate value of that moment. However, the functional side of the same connection, between you and Google, holds the real weight. Here, all your affiliations with New York, similar events, and other connecting variables are assessed, and the result adds to your social media significance and meaning based on how it relates to all your prior actions.

When you learn to combine these contexts, you can generate effective promotion within the digital realm, beyond the reach of the human eye. The website is the place where this can be done most freely. When we talk about differentiation happening in the digital realm, it often refers to showcasing skills specifically in this field.

These links also function internally. Let's imagine you have a storyline on your website that is intended to be published in installments. With each subsequent installment, it's essential to remember to include an internal link to the previous publication. These links not only enhance the reader's experience but also provide valuable information for search engines to process. Each such reaction is, in fact, a statement. If something is valuable, highlight it; if not, don't.

In any case, reinforcing content with associated links or other plug-ins may increase its value. Through the reaction of others you gain external verification and emphasizes you wanting particular attention for something. Without attachment or links something is assumed to be less important. This should be planned carefully. Some artists have a map for the links they have included and why, so they can easily add content and maintain consistency.

If your website is the first result in a search about you, congratulate yourself. This indicates Google values your website as the most authentic source of information about you. You can now leverage potential story-on-story effects more strategically as you are providing the root. All other content will likely be evaluated through that point of view, not the other way around. This should be our destination.

At the same time content made by others increases your capital on social media, the clout. The more external hits allocated to you, your production and your story, usually the better. Promotion facilitation is a puzzle. It should be built brick by brick and step by step so an artist gains sufficient control of their content. However as already mentioned, this isn't always the goal of every artist.

3.4. Areas of Action

The four audiences form the areas of action – where management takes place. Usually, music business is presented through its business areas such as music publishing, recording business, live events, synchronization or merchandise. This is still valid when talking about the business itself and related earning logics. When we change perspective to music business management, which is a wider concept, it is more natural to talk about areas of action. Music is so ubiquitous that it is difficult to have boundaries – especially in modern times. Therefore, these four audiences provide a framework to enable understanding of the essence of music business management, especially from an important strategic point of view. So the above mentioned four audiences can also be considered the areas of action.

Successful management requires smoothly running between and within these areas of action and their interfaces. As important as it is to know your audience, management is also expected to demonstrate the artist's story and the agenda behind it. There remains the need to build business and find an economic meaning for the story and related affiliations. One of the most challenging tasks for management is to discover the financial implications of an artist's story and connect them in a way that generates income for the participants – ideally from multiple income streams or fewer, but sufficiently substantial ones.

Please note the breakdown between different audiences and hence areas of action is conceptual. In reality, a lot of overlapping occurs, which in turn must be taken into account at all stages when operating as a manager.

When an artist succeeds in acquiring fans, it attracts the interest of media and industry. For example an artist might not have a recording agreement, but their own activity acquires new fans daily. As a result, their ranking on streaming services rises, enabling positions in editorial playlists and algorithms offer the artist to new listeners. What is strategically relevant in this situation is the artist's plan. If the artist created this circumstance in order to raise interest with a record company, their reactions will be quite different to one deciding to proceed with their own independent release. Management should be prepared for everything – no plan should be too binding. A back door should be left open for changes of the mind. These kinds of reservations should be included in every decision.

Subsequently, an artist must also decide how to react to inquiries from their other audiences. Media usually calls for different responses than the industry, but there may be overlapping meanings. Many outcomes may require follow-up actions. Prevailing popularity among the public and media may not necessarily convey the right message to the industry. If this is intended to happen, something needs to be done. Or when an achievement within the industry doesn't resonate with the media, it might need to be brought forward in a different manner. Conversely, when your progress and desired outcome require the involvement of others, you can never rely on being understood correctly. Therefore, always ensure everything yourself.

It is important not to inadvertently shut down options by being callous with comments such as an artist wanting to take care of their own career and thereby indicating to labels not to bother contacting them.

Once again, these things may leave a mark on Google. While proceeding with whatever is on the agenda, it is imperative consistency is maintained. Particular attention must be paid to this – especially at the beginning of a career when the online presence isn't yet properly established. Contradicting comments and views will not help an artist's case. In an ideal situation, each new episode supports the past, but also manufactures the future.

3.5. Story Enrichment & Related Episodes

The natural next step is story enrichment, or episodes – depending on the point of view. Story enrichment is usually associated with business and as yet unrealized things, while episodes are about actual events pertaining to an artist. Enrichment takes place either as an action or as a reaction to something that's already happened – as a follow-up. It is absolutely possible for a business objective to only emerge afterwards. The objective of many enrichments is to retrospectively become an episode.

It is important to note that the division of labor is anything but default. The fact someone is an artist manager, doesn't completely describe their tasks. Nowadays, artists are increasingly involved in assisting management, especially when acting independently. Story enrichment is performed by both artist management and the artist, separately and together. Internal protocols dictate how this is carried out. Management uses an artist as a resource in many respects.

Story enrichment could be briefly described as anything that springs out from the story, or the root theme. But it can happen entirely independently, depending on the purpose for which it is carried out. Enrichment has a close connection to intermediation discussed in more detail later in this book. Although enrichment is often perceived as directed towards something new, something that doesn't exist yet, the enrichment does not necessarily require any intermediating activity, but can also be done on the existing activities. For example, enrichment can be productive. When the artist is releasing new music, it increases a size of the catalog and hence an additional source of income for the future. Or an artist issuing their own NFTs. It enables an additional source of income. None of these necessarily require intermediation to happen. Instead, if some operation requires external resources from the third parties, or artist's interest groups, it usually requires intermediation to become true. Consider the artist wanting an interview, it requires intermediation activities when booking them. Story enrichment, or a decision how much you want to exercise intermediation activity, is again, a matter of design – and choice.

The same goes the other way around too. Music & tech allow for opportunities that don't require any intermediation to be realized. An artist may issue NFT's, regarded they have the resources. An artist may take part in social media communities and carry out their business. They may buy their own land in the metaverse and use it as a market place. Some of these are free of charge. It depends how much the artist wants to enrich their story and attached business opportunities.

In order to make a distinction between enrichment and episodes, enrichment is always deliberately formed and consciously included. Episodes may happen without any effort. This is also important to internalize when acting as a manager. One of the main tasks of a manager is to have operative control, which means all self-initiated enrichments should be well-balanced with counterweights – reactive episodes.

Episodes may also include a business perspective, depending on how management reacts to them. One of the ideals in modern music business is to reach the point where related intermediation takes place in reverse. That is, the artist is the one receiving offers and suggestions – where the artist doesn't need to make the invitation. We return to this in the chapter on passive promotion.

Audience reactions can also bring about little surprises and it is up to the artist and their management how to handle this situation. Consider a European artist inputting a large amount of effort to increase their visibility in Europe, but the results are nothing special. Spotify for Artists unexpectedly shows that most streams come from the United States. Instead of finding out why – which is also useful – it makes sense to input effort into expanding in the US. Often US success ultimately reflects on to Europe.

If the artist is still looking for a label – they could try approach US labels instead of European ones. This is a great opportunity from the streaming era. These active operations and related episodes may rock the boat. This is also the reason why this book uses the term story instead of promotion, as you never know from where and how your efforts begin to bear fruit.

Hence, a manager's task is to create favorable preconditions for an artist to succeed – at every stage of their career. We are often dealing with necessities and associated consistency. If a particular success requires preceding actions, they must be taken. This fact should encourage and motivate an artist and their management to engage with consistency in all actions.

Anyone is able to get up-to-date information about you and your activities. In addition, algorithms begin to know how to combine us, our music and the story we want to tell. The better this information is laid out, the better it can be strategically exploited.

For example, we can steer action where the best search engine ranking is. If targeted audiences and others respond to this and react, it will ignite a cumulative effect, which also feeds back to the algorithms, enforcing meaningful connections.

3.6. Preconditions

Up until now, we've largely operated in the digital realm, where online presence is constructed. In the same way as digital preconditions, the physical preconditions are equally vital – those actions we undertake alongside the digital preconditions. I cannot stress enough the importance of this groundwork today. Many agreements come into existence precisely because we've succeeded in handling these preconditions properly, both in the digital and physical realms.

Management's main task is to facilitate. Facilitation can be anything from professional guidance to initializing negotiations and preparing the artist for their future action plan. As the dominant factor is the artist's story, needs and wishes, the manager's influence is relative. At the beginning of a career when the artist is unfamiliar with the business, the manager's key role is to get things running. As a career progresses it is typical the manager's tasks and the division of labor between the artist and manager changes. The starting points of each party in the relationship is also important – the manager is not always the more knowledgeable party. Regardless, preconditions must always be in place for an artist's future operations.

Creating favorable preconditions can involve getting oneself into a state where approaching a contact in this industry will be executed. This can be for example researching the background of such a person and thus having a better understanding of what to talk about.

As reiterated many times, it all begins with a sustainable online presence. Only then is it worthwhile stepping onto the stage of the music business. Only after this does it make sense to engage in physical actions. It's management's task to keep the artist's online presence updated and if the manager enters into the picture where the artist already has an effective online presence, then the task is to adjust it accordingly. If the artist's online presence incomplete, it must be repaired to be in line with current and future needs.

Once this setup is initiated, it can shed light on what to do next. A deeper look can reveal connections. The same happens within a story. There's always something to follow up with – a natural continuum. These are the trails to follow when enriching an artist's story.

Resourceful management always keeps several avenues available in which to operate and stay in motion without the cooperation of others if the actions required for intermediation are somehow stuck.

Sometimes you have to proceed with limited resources. You need to then go through resource by resource and direct actions to where we are strongest.

Let's consider a scenario where the artist is not equipped with a website, and their online presence isn't completely under their control.

This function is carried out by the record label's maintained artist website. Even though this site may accurately represent information about the artist, it is not under the artist's control. When the contract eventually ends, the record label may choose to abandon the site, or alter the content in their favor.

This can be detrimental to the artist if what's left doesn't match with the artist's current position.

An artist has released two albums – including a few singles. Of these releases, information has transferred to search engines. The artist does not have their own homepage, but communication takes place through social media platforms, such as Facebook, Instagram, Tik Tok, or Twitter. Published interviews and critic's reviews are also seen in the results, and various campaigns and missions, for example on Patreon and other artist-to-fan platforms. All connections leave a trace and artificial intelligence of the search engines evaluates their weight in relation to each other. Particular interviews may rank higher because of underlying media clout and depending on the content of that interview dictates whether it is a good or bad thing for the artist.

Although that interview supports the background idea of the artist, all other search results may provide a confusing picture of the artist. The big question here is how the remaining audiences react to this. Does it incite interest in the potential follower or do they leave after a second, does the industry show interest in the artist – are they a time-consuming operation or a potential investment?

If an artist's online presence had been in order before such an operation was launched, the outcome would have been entirely different. All the artist's promotional successes would appear as it should in the artist's search results – further increasing the artist's social media capital in a consistent manner.

One thing to check, if you are new to this. Social media platforms also enable an artist to define themselves. A Facebook page defines you by the description you provide. If you say you are an artist, you are an artist. So, there are many places where an artist may include these related story elements – in descriptions. If there is controversial content between information sources, locate them and correct them. These accidents may be a relic from times when you didn't know what to do. In an ideal situation, your social media platforms, website and official registers of your production metadata provide accurate information about you and input this into AI and its algorithms. This is how to manipulate the image that is seen about you.

Artificial intelligence can assist in maintaining consistency across the board. There's the option of chat – each chat forming its own entity. For example, an artist can create a chat for each of their songs, and likewise for each release and its associated promotion. Whenever the topic comes up in the future, the artist can discuss options within this chat. With a memory trace of all previous conversations, AI can aid the artist in making logical decisions. Then you simply adjust the output to match your style.

Secondly – preconditions may be targeted for a particular mission or measure. Consider an artist releasing new music. The promotion plan contains key interviews and is known in advance, as well as the goals for each interview. It covers how to handle digital service providers (DSP) pitch or some other similar measure. It is management's task to create the conditions for the artist's performance. Once again, internal protocol determines the division of labor, especially with independent artists. Some artists carry out practical interview arrangements themselves, others need a manager or assistant for every task. If the artist has signed a label, label representatives usually lead promotion.

Task-specific preconditions are also involved in negotiations. Intermediary operations regardless of division of labor, are usually led by a manager. Even though instructions and wishes come from the artist, the game plan is from the manager, usually because the manager's field knowledge and experience is more extensive. If this is the case, the manager is responsible for preparing the artist for the related events. At some point the artist will enter negotiations and meet future partners.

The better a manager can explain an action plan and keep an artist up to date on its progress, the easier an artist can perform their part. Conversely, the better an artist is aware of various options and specific features, the easier for them to choose the right partner. Remember, the artist is the one who usually has the final say when it comes to agreements.

Preconditions are about preparing all parties. Consider an action plan with ten potential labels. The manager would take care of contacting the labels with polite invitations of interest, but including the artist as a blind or hidden recipient to keep the artist in the loop with real time information. This transparency gives the artist the possibility to evaluate the content and options and incorporated with manager discussions, the artist is prepared and able to make informed decisions. This is what preconditions are all about and should be practiced whenever necessary. If any matter requires measures prior to completion, this is a universal obligation by management to undertake.

Remember, everything can be tracked and an artist can be followed without being aware. Hence, take this as a friendly reminder. Passive promotion must be arranged in advance to support future promotional prospects, to avoid wasted opportunities. If these features are not enabled, even an expensive campaign can be ineffective, failing to create a story-on-story effect and not increasing social media capital.

It sort of dissipates into thin air, disappearing as quickly as it appeared. Consider an artist inadvertently approaching completely unfit partners, but as a result, knowledge goes to meaningful contacts. With adequate information about the artist, they may approach the artist for further details. Nowadays, these opportunities may occur around every corner without geographical boundaries.

3.7. Passive Promotion

The word promotion is a sum of the parts 'pro' meaning on behalf of and 'motion' meaning movement. Put together this is moving on behalf of something, which is the core meaning of the word we are aiming for – anything that has the effect of enhancing an artist's career is promotion – every single step.

In accordance with its name, passive promotion is such that an artist does not have to do anything once connected as it is self-effective. Passive promotion emanates from an artist's online presence and related unchanging components, such as the story root – as we have already discussed. Passive promotion is set up correctly when it generates accurate and strategically targeted information to meet the needs of our various audiences, all the while considering our own objectives.

It's important to note that our audiences have slightly different needs. For human audiences, including the public, media and industry, what matters is information retrieval and associated references. A well-maintained online presence is an indication of professionalism and can imply many things. However, for search engines and artificial intelligence, the purpose is to generate material to be processed.

Passive promotion, in its visible form, is present on an artist's website, third-party hits, such as interviews and reviews, social media platforms and digital streaming providers. The initial stage, however, is with search engines. If someone doesn't know where to begin to find information about you, they'll Google you. It is of great importance the order of the results. If your homepage is the first hit, it should contain all the relevant links and all the information they require.

Additionally, if someone is interested in your music being in their productions, for example in film, they need to contact you to obtain a license. That information should be available on your website.

Most services nowadays also allow for followers (Spotify, Youtube, Instagram etc). Without having to actively do anything, a notification of your content is automatically sent to them, allowing you to focus on actual content. This has extensive reach and is unsurprisingly one of the primary targets in modern music business – that is, finding your natural audience and gathering them around you.

It could be said that passive promotion is either formal or creative. Platform-related search results are considered formal and can be affected in limited ways dependent on the description options included during initial registration, uploading or through any other recognition technology.

At this point, it is good to note there is a chain between the platforms offering music and the related copyright organizations with their rights-owners. The platforms need licenses to use the music. Royalties and other copyright-related payments are paid to respective rights-holders. A variety of registers, recognition mechanisms and other identifiers are created to serve this purpose. Every play or usage registers in these mechanisms, and based on them, you receive compensation.

The information regarding an artist also has third-party dimensions. This third party information is another layer of passive promotion and its implementation can be quite a creative endeavor.

Let's consider a scenario where an artist needs to secure an interview with a prominent media outlet and the aim of this interview is to highlight a significant aspect. The success of this operation lies in the creative side – how effectively this can be achieved. The strategic significance that may be sought in this context is related to the weight of the media outlet. The more significant the media, the greater its impact. If the artist manages to bring something unprecedented to the forefront in such an interview, it acquires a compelling foundation in the artist's online presence and, subsequently, in passive promotion. Not only does it elevate search results for human audiences, but it also strengthens its content digitally. That particular viewpoint, opinion, or expression of the artist – whatever it may be – starts to be perceived as a 'truth' on a broader scale. Another crucial piece is fitting this into the artist's narrative. It's worth noting that improving online presence through third-party contributions is the management's true art. It always requires the collaboration of others. The way to elegantly execute this operation is the creative part.

3.8. Facilitation of Passive Promotion

Homepages are a great space for facilitating passive promotion. You can present your own arguments of things, strengthen content with the most appropriate links and proceed as a strategy at hand requires. Even better, things do not need to be incorporated immediately and inappropriate items can be removed when their impact ceases. This is the connectedness of passive promotion. Before considering, let's revisit the functional side of the story and bring in a few new observations.

Readable content is what is visible and is intended for the three physical audiences – the public, media and industry. Depending on what is pursued determines the weight and may contain content for all. Sometimes the content has no background motives and are simply episodes. Remember, this is where an artist's intervention can make a difference and highlight meaningful instances for search engines.

The functional part in turn, is linked to the non-physical audience – search engines and their artificial intelligence. It connects content to direct affiliations, but also entices indirect effects. How one uses these is creative and requires finding connections that best support the mission. Its implementation is measured by management's ability to make far-reaching plans.

An essential aspect is your personal experience, significance and connection to the current situation. Suppose you take a group photo of your friends at a gathering where you discuss, let's say, your trip to London. This photo will appear differently to each of you. Everyone has different experiences, meanings and connections to the topic and location of the post. Let's imagine only you have been to London. Such a post resonates with you in a unique way compared to the others, precisely for this reason. Or, consider another post playing a song you've composed. Once again, the post resonates entirely differently to you.

Now, the difference between these two examples lies in copyright. You don't get copyright for your trip to London, but you do for your composed song. Most likely, the post containing your composed music holds greater significance – due to that copyright.

Give weight to what you say by tying it to something valuable, while leaving out what doesn't hold as much significance. This is the design of invisible content.

Therefore, after laying the foundation for your online presence and engaging in open conversations with different audiences, you can leverage this hidden prestige. As you learn to interconnect and consistently present these elements, you enhance the weight of your communication. The caption of each post and how it relates to your personal history is crucial.

If we think completely calculatedly, it would benefit all of us to engage in situations where the caption, location, place and people involved in our posts support our selfish purposes. Each such hit strengthens our social media clout with its significance.

Thus, the most important thing is to ensure that the website is correctly connected to the production, which is the most valuable asset – a permanent thing. Search engines should be able to detect it is really us. With this, we can enrich a story and also include additional attractors to our information.

Strategy is then required to incorporate links to copyright registers, social media platforms or other relevant affiliations within the narrative. Each link has its own background idea and it is imperative each is consistent – not only structurally, chronologically, but also substantively. This is the ultimate design of passive promotion.

Several of these background triggers activate automatically, without a separate connection. If you've previously referenced such an event, mere context or a word in the caption may be enough to hit the mark. Thus, there's a visible and functional aspect to the matter. Many times, this functional aspect is the more critical one. If you already have experience in a certain area or perhaps earned accolades, those are always the strongest references. Think of this as screenwriting, where the idea is to create a story that eventually appears as 'based on a true story.'

You can also include links to song (and phonogram and other production) lyrics on an artist's homepage, for example through LyricFind, to link metadata behind the scenes and provide more information. The overall appearance of a website is like a business card for your operation. Industry can form an opinion of your professionalism when detecting this and noting operations in order, including these indirect effects.

It is possible to highlight important things by linking specific sites – for example if an artist is performing very well on Spotify – however it's important to note these topical issues may change and next month the better performing platform might be Amazon Music and would require updating links.

Links that are not directed to permanent elements, such as copyrights, need continuous monitoring as they may not be permanent. Content may be changed or a link fails and needs correcting. A link map can be a useful tool for this.

Links to third-party content, such as interviews or reviews can be utilized to strengthen an artist's story filling the gaps and thus dictate content on their website.

It is possible to refine or correct comments in interviews by linking the article to an artist's website post or some other location with further comments. With gratitude and comments about the great atmosphere surrounding an interview, an artist can provide context or further input to a topic.

A sequence like this, in turn, could be the next significant storyline in your promotion. Because they resonate with something real – in this case an interview – they inherently carry more weight than content that hasn't materialized yet. It's essential to keep this in mind when executing a promotion.

This interview could serve as a triggering factor for record deal negotiations. When the company sees the artist's success in it, it might be the missing piece in their consideration.

Hence, this functional aspect must be considered in the narrative – knowing when is the right time to introduce something new. We're also interested in probabilities – what are the chances of success for the matter we're bringing up? The general rule of thumb could be that when something becomes confirmed or starts to seem likely, it's the earliest moment to introduce new material.

To summarize, passive promotion is a gateway. Content and consistency to other forums provides information for the three audiences. The more connected to relevant topics, the better their own voice. This also works in reverse where an artist can make a stand by not linking something. You can control much by removing non-existent or outdated links, as well as those providing conflicting opinions to the consistency of one's story. To prime passive promotion allows channelling and utilization of search engine filters to provide the most accurate information surrounding an artist to enhance their story and present this to the three audiences, before someone else does.

Industry likes to monitor what searches turn up on an artist, not just follower numbers and it is appreciated when efforts are put into the area of passive promotion.

There's more to significance with activity in this field. This can also indirectly activate cookies and other alternate push functions and in an ideal situation, the user becomes a follower.

The interface between formal and creative links is not straightforward, but rather a design question of how formal components can confirm creative ingredients and vice versa. Formal links can also include substantive ingredients. Highlighting an artist's new song on their homepage with a formal link may connect to an internal or external website (or both). The internal link takes the reader to the Lyrics section on the artist's homepage, whilst the external link takes the reader somewhere else, for example to where the song stream. Furthermore, there are hyperlinks and other means through which this need can be addressed. Once again, this traffic has meaning to search engines and platforms' AI and algorithms.

When properly used, a homepage can be like a command center for the whole operation. It doesn't matter whether your homepage is the first search result or not. If an artist's Facebook or Instagram page ranks higher, it's sufficient that content is aligned. Third party hits should also be taken into account. Wikipedia has high a search engine ranking and commonly sits at first place in search results, however an artist may not be able to influence this at all. If an artist effectively claims their story through relevant links and other updates in their own forums – it is certainly taken into account when producing a Wikipedia page and as a result, favorable content appears for an artist, itself strengthening the artist's online presence.

This task is learned by doing as you observe results from different actions. A homepage can be edited freely. The aim of the game is to position an artist in a way that appropriately represents their uniqueness – at all career stages. Remember, today's way to stand out is increasingly digital. This requires constant monitoring and a business perspective. If passive promotion intends to boost sales links should be updated to the newest or best performing, depending on the design and current game plan. When the visible aspect corresponds to achievements of the functional side, it's like an unwritten biography for an artist.

3.9. Online Presence & Online Leverage

One thing an artist hopes to achieve in their online presence and related narrative is an interactive response. The more it resonates through responses from various audiences, the greater online leverage an artist ultimately builds. When looking at this completely as the digital identity, the artist's self-perception versus how different audiences perceive the artist over time, we are at the core of the modern ideal. Prevailing popularity, regardless of its nature, should be as extensive as possible, but in an organic way, without forcing it or artificially manipulating. How an artist, with their management, approaches this has a significant impact on how management is carried out.

For example when an artist releases a new song, they hope to generate a lot of user associated content on as many social media platforms as possible. This increases online leverage, not just for economic significance. Additionally, this serves as visible evidence of the artist's activity, its extent and popularity for all audiences.

If everything is set up as planned, an artist's online leverage usually increases over the course of time. Online leverage can be both internal and external. Internal leverage refers to the influence of an artist's own version compared to others. External leverage on the other hand refers to the total number of reactions by others. External leverage is typically affected by seasonal changes. When popularity is at its peak, an artist's has a lot of activity, but when popularity is slower or an artist trends less, reactions are naturally lower in number. In fact, when an artist releases new music, it naturally makes them relevant at that moment. The significant challenge for the artist's management is to keep the artist constantly relevant and actively monitored in a way that aligns with the artist's desires.

An artist management's task is to follow the journey and register achievements. It's the artist's choice which reactions they want to highlight and what to ignore. This is determined again by the action plan in use. It is advantageous to steer attention to where the artist needs it at any given moment, or where it performs the best for current goals.

3.10. Communication

It cannot be overstated how crucial communication between the artist and manager is, especially in the case of its functional and strategic couplings. The artist is the performing body, so on the stage and out in front when it comes to the public and media. The manager, in turn, is the one that communicates with industry and facilitates related operations. If the artist is unaware of relevant links and background strategies, it may lead to inconsistencies and cause serious impediments to well-launched operations.

When an artist produces content on their own social media, they control it and can if necessary correct it. When others are involved, the setting naturally changes. If a journalist hasn't been properly informed about something meaningful, an interview may go awry, but the same applies for the reverse situation where an artist is forced to tend an issue other than what they were expecting in an interview. To avoid horror stories of wasted interviews and consumption of expensive resources, preparation and communication should be held with the utmost importance.

With design and mutual understanding between the artist and manager, situations where an artist can incorporate distinctive points through online presence can be exemplified and these sometimes require well-thought timing to optimize, otherwise opportunities can be lost.

With strategic planning and good communication, ideas can be dropped during interviews and followed up later in social media posts with expansion and clarification. Well-crafted situations will seamlessly connect these two separate incidents in one. These must be based on reality and it is of essence whether a link is related to something that has already happened, or something in the future.

A word of caution on this that when such ideas are highlighted on social media or elsewhere in the media, attention must also be paid to the fact that they may not ever happen. There should always be a plan b, but expectations should be managed to avoid things appearing as failures if they don't work out. An artist repeatedly mentioning rocking out stadiums, but gigs take place in small clubs does not necessarily support their strategy and will appear so in the eyes of audiences.

The importance of communication and transparency is paramount in the industry. When everyone is informed and aware of intentions then people can work together to achieve what everyone wants. Things usually break down at some point in discussions when there is a miscommunication or failure to properly inform all parties.

In an ideal situation, the artist is on board at every step of the way. This way they also participate in promotion strategically. The better informed an artist is of background motives, especially the game plan and its realization, the easier it is to incorporate in their own activities. For example, guiding people to visit their social media and bring them under the influence of their passive promotion. As the frontline an artist needs to be aware of content and objectives to more accurately implement their side of activities. A private Facebook or WhatsApp group to share relevant information is a good way to do this.

Communication is important, especially at the beginning of a manager relationship. When parties consider their potential collaboration, they do it together. Many communication tools like WhatsApp offer voice message capabilities. You can start the conversation by talking about values and the other person doesn't have to respond immediately. If there's a lot of conversation, you can listen at double speed. In this process, you gain more firsthand knowledge about the other person and can assess the meaningfulness of the collaboration from different perspectives. The artist-manager relationship is a trust relationship, often aiming for long-term cooperation. Due to the intensity of collaboration, it's not always wise to rush into it hastily.

However, remember one thing: when you communicate online, avoid sharing your most intimate details or any information you wouldn't want others to know. This way, you can prevent potential issues if something happens to your account.

3.11. Active Promotion

The implementation of passive promotion is retrospective in nature. It occurs around events and episodes that have already happened and thus it is natural to talk about the four audiences that you create and produce content for. Switching perspective to the business side of matters, the story enrichment – these things haven't happened yet, but are to be pursued. Then there are the four areas of action with the core intention to actively connect business to the story. When accomplished, it's another source of passive income – just like passive promotion.

Business is mainly focused on the public as they are the ultimate paying source from which money flows. This is called the b-to-c sector, or the business to consumer.

Another area of action is b-to-b sector, or business to business. Please note that industry is not limited to the music business, but all other industries. For example, if our music ends up in a movie, the film's producer is in charge of the compensation we receive. Or if an advertiser wants to use music in their ads, they are responsible for making sure rights have been obtained correctly.

If the music already exists, this becomes passive income and we don't have to do anything except grant the necessary rights and name the price. If the music doesn't exist or will be custom made, action is required for monetization and the artist will be paid on completion of the product.

On the operational side, industry is the place for strategic support and other resources such as funding. Usually their need varies at different stages of a career. We will return to this particular subject in the chapter Contracts and Copyright.

The remaining areas of action are mainly for marketing and promotional purposes. People tend to mix up the words marketing and promotion. Promotion is done almost everywhere – it isn't only tied to results with some particular objective. If you enhance prospects while facilitating improvements in passive promotion, this is promotion. If you create a marketing campaign for your next release, that's also promotion. Anything that makes conditions better for future prospects is considered promotion. What separates promotion from marketing are the costs. Marketing almost without exception requires a budget, while promotion can be performed without monetary resources. Additionally, promotion isn't always strictly about increasing economic gain, whilst marketing usually is.

Only rarely can an artist request money for an interview. Usually it's the other way around and often an artist hires a publicist or promotion representative to acquire these interviews. Awareness, subsequent improvement of online presence and creating new episodes are aimed at enhancing business prospects. The ultimate intention is to create a story amidst a continuation that creates economic meaning. For example, if an artist's social media or media appearance attracts the public to listen to their music, the operation can be said to be a success. Such measures are continue as a series, with the idea of maintaining a continuum.

An example illustrating the evolution of business is that things aren't always as they seem. Within the same set of tasks, there are often dual meanings or double entendres. A publicist can be used, for example, in building one's own organization during a release. While the publicist promotes the artist's new release, management leverages that visibility to showcase the artist's activities, perhaps to a booking agency they are seeking to collaborate with.

The same can be said of search engines. The main rule is to not stop optimizing these settings until the online presence has a life of its own, meaning the public, media and industry learn of an artist and link it to the artist's work without searching.

It is about positioning an artist to bring in not only economic results, but also story-related awareness. This is the setting from which all operations are ultimately produced. How fast an artist reaches this goal is individual, but it's also good to note that not all artists seek the highest level of popularity and money.

The ideal of modern music business and the existence of copyright is to strive for passive income over active income. Passive income such as royalties, bring income to an artist and their manager according to how well music performs on digital streaming services and other platforms, or how much their music is used in commercial b-to-b purposes. Actions behind these should be continued until passive sources of income are sufficient for an artist to be independent – also economically. When this stage is reached, the artist then chooses how much energy is needed for active operations at any given time.

Recent world events have shown that active promotion may be prevented by self-influential factors. In order to be able to fully act in a disadvantageous situation it is good to have reserves. Passive promotion is a means for an artist to proceed even without active promotion.

Seasonal fluctuation is part of the music business. If the story and its episodes cease to produce passive income and promotion pace slows down, additional enrichment is usually needed. Often times, enrichment is directly connected to story episodes. Releasing new music acquires a new episode for a story, but also a business-related element. If the public and b-to-b sector provide financial appreciation, the journey can go on.

At some stages, the artist's story, strategic content and artistic credibility are things to embrace. In other stages, economic objectives are the center of attention. How much flexibility is required or the need for compromises depends on the current action plan, its goals and resources available. Not all artists want to be active and making money all the time and it's important management takes note of this.

If an artist's cash flow and other financial resources doesn't enable implementation of their plans, something needs to be done. Instead of creating new episodes through new releases, there are other options such as finding advertisers to provide industrial collaboration. Special attention should be put into determining how much time such a project would require and how likely the success in negotiating it.

If an artist acquires an advertising agreement, it should be seriously thought how it affects the existing story, future episodes, or if it may irritate audiences. It may not be worth it, especially if it is inconsistent with an artist's values. A good collaboration is one that suits both the artist and advertiser. Consider also if such an operation is too time-consuming and may compromise other important activities. If the artist is in the early stages of their career, a long silence isn't good as fans will expect regular activity. If such a project takes half a year and the artist is unreachable throughout that time, it may not be an ideal solution. These things should be taken into account.

The same is true with recording agreements. Acquiring one is important, but you cannot ignore ongoing operations and have them lag behind. One of the most important tasks of management is to anticipate the future whenever possible and map out relevant variables. One major variable in everything is the construction of a competent team and the different motives involved. Another important task is to monitor how well the operation itself is performing.

One thing to keep in mind across the board is that when we talk about active promotion, it's more about the continuous movement and its sustainability rather than individual actions. Not everything needs to be connected to the internet and things hidden away often end up there sooner or later if they have significance. A strategically built online presence with its related effects of passive promotion takes care of this. So, instead of constantly trying to create something meaningful, sometimes it's better to just do what feels natural. It's not uncommon for a photo taken by an artist on their vacation to resonate the most, creating a more significant business effect than actual promotion.

It should be pointed out that even though live performances are a crucial operational point and a source of income for many artists, they are not specifically addressed in this book. It is assumed that most of you are familiar with this subject already, and not all artists want to perform live. If earnings are based solely on live appearances without their own releases, this becomes more about musicians than artists. To be an artist requires releases. Additionally, artists in the future may perform exclusively in the metaverse.

One more thing: you will notice how important spontaneous interaction in the field is. When we talk about active promotion, this aspect cannot be ignored. So, you don't always need to have a big business idea in mind when you contact people in the industry. The more you move in this environment, the better you start to internalize the crucial unwritten rules and industrial practice.

Conversely, it's advisable for artists to engage in all sorts of interactions with their audiences and fans. Each such interaction may bring not only a new fan but also a potential new storyline.

3.12. Motives

Before we enter the world of contracts and copyright, a few words about motives. This has a huge impact on team building and is one of management's main tasks. Team building always takes place through contracts and the related copyright is the thing that ties them together. The more each participant is involved in the copyright areas, the more solid the connection to an operation. Conversely, the looser the strings, the more important to find some other motivation.

This is a great point regarding a specific detail. As we've discussed, the story root of an artist always involves copyrighted production, composition and/or recording. It's what starts to define artists – managers have their own story root, although it manifests differently and isn't as original as copyright. The story root of a manager, however, is always derivative.

The manager's involvement in the artist's activities is the manager's story root. This doesn't necessarily come into existence just by the manager signing a managerial agreement with the artist. However, it can happen that way – as long as it is verified in a way recognized by search engines. When such an event is permanently recorded online, affecting algorithms and/or artificial intelligence mechanisms, it becomes a form of credit.

As the manager performs their role, certain aspects of the management likely become more valuable than others. A strategic aspect in one's resume is to emphasize certain tasks over others. It's also essential to consider risk management. When a managerial relationship is in its early stages and its duration is unknown, making grand claims about its existence might not be advisable.

Therefore, a manager often claims ownership of management at the moment when some real success has actually occurred or the operation starts to become professional.

At this very moment, these hits begin their defining task; the search engine gradually starts forming an image of the person as a manager and eventually defines them as such. It's important to note that this is often a much longer process than that for an artist, as a manager lacks the support of copyrights in this context. The manager doesn't inherently possess anything original and it originates from the success within another person's operation and under their copyrights – in this scenario, the artist's. What matters significantly to the manager is the binding agent that connects them to the artist and the artist's story. This serves as a powerful reminder about copyrights; in their case, the definition begins automatically the moment something is published – and it doesn't require the involvement of others.

Consequently, the first point that should be considered when talking about motives is the position of each party or team member regarding copyright. Everyone has their rights based on their position and it varies from originator to financial derivatives and/or relevant authority. Note that members can be both individuals and companies and that motives can differ between a company and its employees.

For example, the music publisher usually has administrative rights, that is, control over the songs in the music publishing agreement. They can control granting rights for the music and also receive a share in economic results. The record company, in turn, owns the master recording, or at the least partnership. They control how the master is used commercially and a share in financial gains. This is logical and straightforward and both industrial bodies have motives for financial incentives and appeasing artistic standards. However, this is not necessarily the case when considering employees of these companies in the equation.

Consider an A&R (Artist & Repertoire) manager working for a company for three years. They already know what to do and what can be achieved. They have profit responsibility for their own roster, with a goal to succeed with most artists. This is the corporate goal. Within or outside can be personal motives. Promotion within the company or even moving to a competing label. Such motives likely to influence overall performance.

These parallel motives can be realized without distracting from company goals, but if such personal motives interfere, something probably must be done. In this situation, the biggest difficulty is unpredictability. Many factors can influence how this turns out; record company employees have the advantage of a monthly salary despite everything. In addition, music publishers and record labels have shares in their artists' copyright revenues through their contracts. For them, breaks may not be relevant, whereas an artist, especially in the early stages of their career, needs continuous movement and the associated income. A prolonged standstill in this sector can also hinder operations elsewhere.

The same can happen also closer to home with an artist's manager's life situation changing and requiring a more substantial or reliable income from the percentage of the artist's proceeds. This may cause problems and adjustments will need to be made.

There are many options to solve this, for example by representing additional artists, perhaps only temporarily if things go well for the main artist. Commission percentages can also be renegotiated or temporary solutions put in place.

Hopefully a mutually agreeable situation can be settled upon to suit the needs of everyone involved in the journey.

Those with no right to copyright revenue and hence passive income are always in the weakest position. Their income is connected to future activities the artist still needs to perform. If they are cancelled, they receive nothing. Music publishers' and record companies' position on the other hand, allow them to generate revenue even if an artist ceases their career. This may also apply to the manager if their agreement contains post-termination considerations. An artist's agent is in a completely different situation where their income is based on the artist's activities. If the need arises for more profitable appearances to support an agent's income needs, then revaluation and adjustments may be necessary.

Motives are not necessarily due to mere circumstances, but also a question of choice. Personal missions and goals also impact these choices and the ground work should be laid early in one's career to support these.

For many in the industry, no matter the actual position, accomplishing goals is about sacrifices – how much you are willing to invest for the dream. This all comes together through individual actions – some work on a day-to-day basis and others alongside their own day job. Not all members are available at the same time, which requires coordination of meetings. This can slow things down, especially in the beginning when setting up the organization and the commencement of operations are still in progress.

Discrepancies may also arise from copyright ownership issues. It takes time and resources until an operation becomes financially viable. It is better if the copyright owner finances the operation and considers the investment (time or otherwise) of others.

When building a team, you should try map out each party's motives. There is no one-size-fits-all solution, as every configuration in the music business is unique, although details can be balanced and result in a result that motivates all participants.

Managing motives, especially those that pop up to rock the boat without notice, requires monitoring to ensure things proceed as planned and run smoothly, correcting the course where required.

3.13. Monitoring

If an artist's organization is professionally managed, it increases credibility among all its audiences. A well maintained online presence, shows an artist is active. Monitoring is how one keeps tabs and follows developments, making updates when needed.

There are many reasons why an artist's online presence doesn't resonate as it should. First, an artist's popularity isn't constant or a given. It requires constant attention – especially when the actions do not yield the desired results. Second, search engines continuously evaluate the internet and today, AI is constantly training itself. It is quite possible that things that were in order a month ago, aren't anymore. Management needs to be awake.

For example, revisit the artist hoping for a recording agreement where something put them on the label's radar. But when the company researches the artist they fail to find anything that supports further collaboration. This is why passive promotion should be the first thing undertaken before starting any operations. You should also refresh your online presence from time to time as in an ideal world search results provide the most topical results about an artist.

Monitoring is not just for the optimization of online presence. A manager needs to monitor the progress of overall image, public awareness and economic development. Many factors are relevant to running a promotion.

There may be a need to temporarily diverge from the main story and here, monitoring is paramount. Time away should be minimal. For example an artist starts a Patreon campaign to acquire capital – it can be anything from issuing NFT collectibles, avatars or launching new merchandise. This needs attention to get traction, but when needs are sufficiently met then it's time to return to the original narrative.

There may be multiple concurrent goals and a well maintained online presence emphasizes these. If an artist is selling tickets to a tour, selling locations should come first. When the tour is sold out or ticket sales reaches a sufficient level, it is time to move onto a new objective.

In the midst of constant ongoing operations, the root theme and an artist's overall image, an artist may still have other long-term plans such as acquiring a recording agreement. These concepts need to be aligned.

Engagement rate of both followers and subscribers should also be monitored and optimized wherever possible and also continuously assessed for their effectiveness. This also applies to paid promotion. Resource availability also impacts these decisions and actions, and necessitates a few words about exits.

When an artist acquires resources from elsewhere than primary revenue generating operations, usually sacrifices are made along the lines of operational constraints, such as partial or complete forfeit of control. These internal arrangements within the industry have their own logic. With interest groups wanting sole exclusive rights, which is sometimes justified and for the benefit of an artist, there is always a chance things do not succeed as planned. For this purpose, there are exits.

Before we move to the second part of this book, a few comments. It is possible to acquire arrangements without loss of ownership and control, eg. through advertising. On completion of a campaign or cooperation, the artist is compensated and the situation is restored to its original setting. Money is also not the only resource. Strategic knowledge relevant to an artist's success may impact agreement acquisition. An artist may give up many of their rights with a recording agreement, however in return they may receive a faster and more effective way to get closer to their goals.

Not all artists want to be independent. For some, economic and artistic freedom is what they ultimately aim for. There are hybrid solutions between these two extremes and for example if an artist doesn't want to give up on some particular right or freedom, it can be excluded from the agreement.

4. CONTRACTS

4.1. Contract Management

It is completely a matter of taste which is brought up first – contracts or copyright – they are closely related. I'll start with Contracts, although we also use the term Agreements.

Before contract content and issues affecting them are dealt with more closely, we must revisit the basics of music business management for a moment. Before any agreement is considered, it is worth mapping their true need. Music business agreements are long-term and exclusive – you don't want to sign a recording agreement just because it sounds cool to have one.

Contract management is the tactical side, with a wide range of contracts within the music business. If you grant the rights to something, it is probably binding, which can be either good or bad. You can make almost any kind of arrangement to benefit your rights, but you may forfeit them more than necessary.

Copyright is the technical side and is on the basis of your contribution. If your contribution entitles you to copyright, it is yours. This may change through contracts. Rights management of copyright is similar to contract management for contracts.

Together, contracts and copyright form the tools for conducting business. For this reason, they need to be thoroughly understood – at least in their essential aspects.

It should be emphasized that while contract management primarily pertains to existing valid agreements, it must be taken into account even during the negotiation phase of contracts.

The better one can incorporate their own requirements during the negotiation phase and consequently into the contract, the easier the contract management will be also in the future.

Agreements usually apply to resources you don't have or things you don't want to deal with yourself, such as production and operative costs, strategic knowledge in copyright administration or marketing, or existing infrastructure for making these objectives happen. The most prominent industrial partners are naturally the labels for recorded music and music publishers for song management.

Contracts must also be addressed when acting deliberately on an independent basis, without rights-transferring industrial support for those who want it. If the artist uses aggregates to distribute their music, the agreement with CD Baby or DistroKid is a similar thing to pay attention. There are also many companies providing services for artists to find a partner most suited to a situation or objective and its implementation, however in this chapter, we will go through agreements relevant to industrial partners.

Time is of utmost importance in contracts. At too early a stage, it is not worthwhile giving up shares. The question that needs answering is the true need of the external help and how long for. Contracts should also be monitored for relevance, content and compliance, like other areas of activity. If they fail to be relevant they should be altered or find a new solution. An artist's plan and surrounding conditions determine the right move to make at any given time.

Correctly functioning management maps all available resources and assesses who will bring in what resources. Back up plans in case of problems are also accounted for. We already talked about motives. Contracts should not be taken for granted, no matter how obvious settings seem.

Agreements safeguard your position. Premature agreements don't think further than the lack of financial value in initial phases, but this illusion may become expensive. Nowadays the possibility for a song to become an overnight viral sensation is a reality. All it takes is one Tik Tok influencer and a song can spread everywhere, resulting in a snowball effect and increase in streaming volume.

Such an opportunity is yet another reason to ensure that your production is correctly linked to music pay sources. Many of these plays generate revenue automatically, meaning every success reflects in your bank account with a delay. If you haven't linked yourself to these pay sources, that money will be left on the table.

Copyright applies to your own involvement and each rights-owner of a song has their own personal right to their contribution and its independent use. If an artist initially intended to be part of a band, but no agreement reached, members can independently jump off the carriage and make use of the accrued popularity for their own self-intent and purposes. On the other hand a member can decide their contribution shouldn't be used, resulting in the whole work remaining unpublished or unreleased. Contracts are needed to eliminate such possibilities.

Contract management's task is to ensure the economic value of copyright is equal for all. Financial losses are not the only thing at stake, but also smooth continuation towards a common goal. If a member decides to leave the group after initial success, many things have to be reimagined and started again from the beginning.

I'll return to copyrights, but for now this was intended to demonstrate the importance of an agreement in advance.

4.2. Resource Acquisition

Contract management is the tactical side of things. When observing true objectives behind agreements, it usually revolves around resource acquisition – for the artist. For industry, it is about making a profit. The important questions are how much outside help is needed and for how long, with consideration to the fact that profit isn't everything.

If an artist strives for independence, but requires outside help, they should stick with the contract until the designated target is reached. Once this is reached, an artist no longer requires the contract and this should be kept in mind during contract management, before putting names on any agreement.

Some agreements are made for a unit, whilst others for an organization's internal relations. If a band signs a recording agreement, the contract is for the whole band with all members as the signing party, after which they act as a unit.

The first thing to consider is to map out how far you can travel on your own resources and define the upper limit, that is when progression on your own is no longer possible. This is useful when considering external support and its need. Its meaningfulness and relationship to goals. Sometimes it is more sensible to give up on some of your rights when the realization of something important requires.

It is possible to make significant headway as an independent. However, if your ambition is to be one of the greatest, you will probably have to partner with a Major label or their subsidiaries, as they have the infrastructure required.

The terms for when to take certain opportunities are unique. An emerging artist, whose market position is not yet solidified may have weaker terms than those with an already established market position. The million dollar question is when is the right time to start actively striving and for how long is it reasonable to fly with your own wings.

Time can also be of essence. Although resources might be sufficient, something may move the target beyond a reasonable time span. Thus external resources may be enlisted. It is typical that an artist doesn't want to sign a music publishing agreement, instead taking care of publishing themselves. This would require establishing their own publishing company, which is a heavily time-consuming operation and they also have to learn the whole business, making separate agreements with relevant copyright organizations and related administration – this takes time. To that end, there are Collective Management Organizations (CMOs).

That is, Songtrust or other collective management organizations can be utilized. They usually charge 15 percent and you keep 85 percent. Songtrust also doesn't take any copyright ownership of your songs or creative control. You can also choose which songs are included and agreements are usually limited. Thus you can easily terminate an agreement for better arrangements in the future.

You should also consider familiarizing yourself with The Mechanical Licensing Collective. It provides valuable information, and by joining, you can secure representation for mechanical royalties from streaming services. Your task is to find the solution that best suits you.

In addition to mechanical royalties, an artist is entitled to performance royalties. For this purpose, there are PROs (Performance Rights Organizations) such as ASCAP or BMI. To fully access royalties, the artist needs to join both.

It is your decision – is it reasonable to go it alone, or wiser to input money for the task to be effectively managed.

In addition to benefits, contracts also include constraints and it is important to have clear exits if things don't go as planned. As already mentioned, many agreements involve exclusivity. For example an artist signed with a recording company cannot do recordings with other companies. This is valid until the agreement is terminated.

An artist may also become dependent on the record company's contribution and an artist may become stuck even in the face of a company not maintaining its responsibilities. This will likely affect other areas of an artist's activities and the original purpose of the agreement remains unfulfilled.

Plan B's such as exits are for such situations. Including conditional mandates within a contract can also allow continuation without its complete termination. When a current goal ceases to exist, or the circumstances change an alternative arrangement provided in the terms of the agreement is switched to.

Consider marketing obligations attached to a recording agreement where a record company must foot the bill and produce three promotional videos for an artist, with half considered an advance that the company is entitled to recoup from the artist's future royalties. At some point they realize they no longer need these videos and the money would be better spent on tour support. If the contract has conditions included, it does not even have to change.

There are many ways to incorporate different exit strategies in agreements so that everyone wins. It's important to maintain a balance in this situation, or it can easily lead to problems down the road. The party that lacks a financial incentive in the contract typically becomes passive, especially if the contract has become an unpleasant experience.

Let's consider a music publishing agreement. Let's assume that the artist, as a songwriter, also performs their own music. The artist enters a recording agreement with an entity that also manages music publishing. Thus, two contracts are signed, one for recording and another for music publishing. The interval between releases can be used to dictate when an agreement concludes, such as when the artist releases their next album. This is one option. Other options are a specific number of years and after this time period ends, music publishing rights are returned to the artist.

From the artist's perspective, both options seem favorable. The agreement continues only with active cooperation and when it ends, the music publishing also ends. If the artist includes a provision that allows rights to revert to them, for example, ten years from now, everything should be fine. This is undoubtedly true if everything goes well. What if it doesn't, though? What if the recording falls short of its target and there's also no use for the music outside of that original context? This situation leads to a deadlock, where both the recording agreement and the music publishing agreement need to be reevaluated. If the artist's partner, both as a record company and a music publisher, has made a significant financial investment and the terms are at this level, they may not have the incentive for further contributions. Without an exit strategy or an alternative solution, the artist might remain in limbo until a specific provision or condition in the contract releases them.

Time is not the only thing to focus on – an artist should not relinquish their rights more than the purpose of a contract and related partnership requires. A music publishing agreement shouldn't go beyond that and should only pertain to songs the artist has written for this purpose, not other songs outside that scope, or for other artists to record. The case is quite different for situations where the artist only acts as a songwriter, not a performer of songs. In these cases, the whole idea is to offer the songs for other artists to record.

A word of caution that examples are for understanding matters only. Ensure all agreements are seen by a lawyer. As you should always do with agreements. If there is no reason for something, don't do it. Copyright is at stake and you do not want to make mistakes. Also, remember a music publishing agreement is a separate entity from a recording agreement, not to be dealt with in the same agreement.

4.3. Price of Contract

When resources are settled and the way in which they will be obtained is clear, a contract is then determined by price with the artist's share usually paid in royalties. That is, the amount an artist receives when granting rights to their copyrights in exchange for the resources they receive to pursue their economic and artistic goals.

For industrial partners such as recording companies or music publishers, the most important goal is to establish a position with regard to the artist's copyright, usually involving some kind of ownership, or at least control over use. The general rule is the more extensive financial responsibility, the greater their position is. Remember, it doesn't always have to go this way. A small variable in the equation may give you a reason to think differently about the situation.

The correct value of both parties' input should be taken into account. Naturally, copyright is an artist's most valuable asset, but other factors such as social media presence and followers, or successful passive promotion set up also impact their weight. The more resources an artist can stake, the bigger their royalties.

Determining royalties is one of the hardest tasks. Conditions may change over time with assets losing or increasing in value. It is important that a contract leaves room for reviewing the terms of the contract as needed. In an ideal situation, an agreement enables modifications to maintain balance. Music business agreements are characterized by long-term vision and subject to unprecedented futures. Both parties should feel comfortable with the position they have in an agreement.

Consider an artist succeeds with their first album allowing them to produce followup albums, partly with their own resources. An agreement should enable this and introduce a variety of opportunities pre-agreed to prepare for necessary changes. In such a situation, the type of recording agreement would change from traditional, in which the label is responsible for all costs, to a master agreement with larger royalties for the artist. The best case scenario would enable the artist to be a co-owner of the master recordings. How easy or difficult to get such conditions is another thing.

There are always other options. It is possible rights-transferring is completely omitted from an agreement, instead a licensing agreement is arranged where the record company receives the same rights as a traditional agreement but through a license, not ownership.

It's always advantageous for an artist to release their music through a licensing agreement. This way, they retain a larger financial share and more decision-making power, at least initially. If we revisit the earlier concept of needs-based thinking, artists could consider the following approach: In the early stages of their career when the necessary resources aren't readily available, they might opt for a traditional record deal. As their career gains momentum, they could transition to releasing music through licensing agreements after the second album. By the time the third album comes around, the artist is more self-sufficient and doesn't require external support in the same way. Of course, this is an oversimplified scenario and how to practically manage this transition is another matter. The intention here was to illustrate the complexities related to needs-based considerations.

Not all music business agreements establish ownership, such as those with a manager, who usually receives a percentage of income in the form of a commission, as the contract determines. If a manager agreement even hints on transfer of rights related to copyright, something is wrong. If such rights are to be transferred between artist and manager, it must be done in another capacity, such as also being a music publisher or label for the artist.

4.4. Rights & Obligations

Copyright ownership is not the only trading good with respective industrial partners, control is also agreed. Before rights and obligations are reviewed more closely, it should be noted that ownership and control does not always go hand in hand.

In case of a music publishing agreement, an artist as a songwriter receives a bigger share of the profits of their respective catalog and if a publisher maintains control, the publisher decides how to exploit the catalog commercially and factually. The publisher decides whether to accept offers to use the music. For songwriters this can be a delicate matter – not just financially – as they may not want their music connected with certain things. If it is clear in advance these situations may arise, conditions must be made so an agreement could exclude certain situations. This should be addressed before entering into an agreement.

With regards to manager agreements, the artist and manager should have it explicitly explained what the manager is able to do on behalf of the artist. The manager's position is derivative throughout. The agreement may state a manager can accept limited types of offers, but for many tasks, the manager needs prior approval from the artist.

The purpose of agreements requires clarification of terms and conditions for designating rights and obligations of the parties concerned. In an ideal situation, there is counterbalance between give and take, and each party carries out their own responsibilities, with emphasis on accuracy to avoid unnecessary conflicts and disagreements.

Everything should be mentioned specifically and covered in an agreement. Conditions should cover every tiny detail whenever possible. If an artist has their own YouTube channel it should be considered what happens with it after signing a recording contract, as usually a recording label releases the music through their own channel. Conditions can be made for this, for example. The artist can keep their YouTube channel and the music included in it up to that point. However, new music recorded by the artist while the agreement is in effect will primarily be released through the company's channel. The big question is whether the artist can also include this new music on their own channel. If they can, this could be a significant financial advantage to the artist. Every situation is different, and many factors influence the decision.

Similarly if an artist has worked hard to increase their subscribers and the financial value is significant, this should not be given away with an agreement. No one should benefit from someone else's hard work for free. Things need to be specifically considered such as what happens at the end of the agreement period and whether fans prefer the artist's own channels for releases.

An artist can always use their holdings as a trading chip. Temporarily giving up (even partially) rights can acquire better conditions in contracts. The more extremes and abnormalities from the norm, the more cautious you should be. Always consider the plan and goals.

The same goes for expenses. An artist should avoid obligations that may give rise to costs without justification.

Expenses can behave in many ways. In some situations, expenses remain the responsibility of the payer, while in other situations, expenses can be recouped, either fully or partially, from the party on whose behalf they were paid. The most ambiguous expense reimbursement mechanism is related to expenses for which a mathematical value is assigned in the contract, but their execution is far from it. In this situation, the payer can take care of a task, even in their own studio, almost for free. When this end product is then used for the common good, the price defined in the contract is applied.

Artists can be made financially responsible for promotion, either entirely or in part. In reality, a press release is sent on their behalf. If a mathematical value is assigned to such an action and it doesn't match the reality, additional profit is generated at the expense of the artist within an existing business. Similar artificial cost structures can be created in various ways. From the artist's perspective, such practices are at least initially questionable. It becomes even more questionable if the decision-making authority for these actions shifts away from the artist.

Of course, other factors can influence the situation and certain terms of the contract may favor such a solution for the artist. However, if you come across such terms, alarm bells should ring.

4.5. Post-Termination Effect

Contracts for music business tasks or assignments are set in place and typically fees are paid with delay or impact at a later date. Also, copyrights have a relatively long protection period, making them a valuable and far-reaching asset. In light of this, post-termination terms need to be negotiated. Post-termination clauses give incentives to make an agreement, otherwise no one would ever make investments.

To clarify, here, the post-termination effect refers to additional rewards, not the typical conditions in agent agreements, for example. This means everything resulting in some kind of reward will be compensated somehow at some point in time – for example a year post agreement.

Post-termination clauses are all individual and agreed upon by each party on a case-by-case basis. Sometimes agreements have none, whilst others last an equal length of time post-termination. For example management that has lasted three years may continue to receive equal compensation the following three years. If a full commission for that whole period feels too much, it can be agreed to decrease it on a statement-by-statement basis, with the first statement being 75% of the full amount, the second 50% and the final one, for example, 25%.

It is particularly important to note that in copyright transfer agreements, such as record and music publishing contracts, certain sections of the agreement remain in effect even if active engagement between the parties ceases. For instance, in the contract the record label holds the rights acquired to trade the catalog created by the artist during the contract's validity. Conversely, the record label pays royalties to the artist for as long as they receive revenue from the music recorded by the artist during the term of the agreement.

In record contracts, there are other residual effects as well. One of the standard clauses in record contracts is a five-year non-compete clause for the songs that the artist has recorded for the label during the contract period. The artist is restricted from re-recording these songs until five years have passed after the termination of the contract. Due to several incidents in the industry, especially in those contract proposals, longer prohibitions in this regard are beginning to appear. When these commonly used terms are used as examples, it's important to remember one thing – one is not obliged to agree to them and they can always be negotiated.

Post-termination clauses may allow labels to recoup costs they have put into an artist's accomplishments. These should all balance out so that each input receives its due compensation.

One more time, even though this book includes examples related to contracts from here and there, you don't necessarily need to follow them literally. That is, you don't have to act according to them but rather be aware of their existence. So you can implement contract management in a way that you feel is best for each situation.

From the artist's perspective, of course, it is recommended to limit the possibility of recouping to the active part of the contract. Such a restriction can help protect the artist's future earnings and ensure that the artist begins to benefit from their music without a continuing financial burden. As a professional entity in the music industry, the record label would be expected to assess its business risks through alternative means within the contract.

4.6. Manager Agreement

4.6.1. Definitions

The first thing to address is the true essence of the manager's agreement. Meaning, what is different to typical manager agreements. A manager isn't a manager in the typical sense.

In the music business a manager is often seen as a CEO (chief-executive-officer), responsible for their actions to the owner, the artist, as managers elsewhere, however there's a twist. As the copyright owner, the artist usually has the final say. Normally, a CEO has authority to sign agreements, but in the music industry this is rarely the case. Recording agreements, music publishing agreements are for an artist to sign – despite the fact that an artist's activities can be carried out in a corporate form. Since copyright is the most prominent asset, the manager's role as CEO is more limited. A manager has power-of-attorney, but mainly for routine business operations. Additionally, even though an artist acts in a corporate capacity, copyright is owned individually by its members, with copyright assets provided for company use. If the company ceases to exist, nothing in relation to copyright changes. Copyright is the thing that dictates – or at least should – the content of everything.

4.6.2. Objectives

The core objective of a manager agreement is to arrange an artist's internal organization. Teaming up with music business bodies is usually just a wise thing to do. The division of labor and jurisdictions is seen in an agreement, but there's no one-size-fits-all solution here, with each artist a unique configuration. Nowadays, independent artists more frequently take care of management themselves, acquiring managers for particular assignments or tasks, while the artist remains in the CEO position. Like in other areas of action, resource acquisition and current needs dictate terms. A manager operating on a case-by-case basis may change roles to an artist's day-to-day manager.

In an ideal situation, the artist and manager have mutual motive and become one. Because the story of an artist and related business is imperative, a manager's personal preferences no longer exist. All activities put the artist's interests first. A manager needs to consider this and their own motives before taking on an assignment, especially if day-to-day management is concerned. Providing permission to have your name associated with an artist comes with the responsibility of being completely accountable for all tasks and current needs of an artist. No matter the content of an agreement – that's the way the industry sees this.

If it is clear in advance that you will not be working across all the compartments of management, it is a good idea to make it explicit. If the artist has a business manager taking care of the artist's already secured assets, then it lacks enrichment. This should be clearly stated so that the industry understands it. This way, the industry knows how to contact the artist's operational management for their matters and the business manager for their respective matters.

Engagement and devotion are also important aspects of management. It is typical a manager also takes on other capacities in order to get things started, especially early on in an artist's career. Accepting these conditions can result in a successful career as a manager.

Sometimes a specific management person is not appointed at all, to avoid ambiguity in an artist's external communication. Additionally, this way, your name and involvement won't be prominently featured as the primary responsibility holder, but rather as part of the management team. By doing so, you're also safeguarding your reputation. This is advisable, especially at the beginning of the management relationship when credits aren't yet established and the meaningfulness of the collaboration is still untested. Contact info could simply be

Management: management@artist.com

with access to those it may concern. Then internal protocol dictates who replies to inquiries.

This method can also be utilized for specific contacts, such as;

For Sync&Licensing: sync@artist.com

music supervisors then know who to approach if for example they want an artist's music for a film.

At this point, it's essential to take special notice, especially if you're operating independently or at a stage in your career where you haven't entered into record or music publishing agreements. If you've created the music yourself and own both the music and the related recordings, make sure to mention this. By doing so, you're conveying valuable information to music supervisors when they express interest in your production. When such information is readily available, you enhance your chances of securing sync placements in audiovisual productions like movies, TV series, commercials, or games.

4.6.3. Manager's Own Position

A manager should consider their stance before accepting any assignment and evaluate their own resources and willingness to commit to the coming work load. If a manager foresees limited availability, there is still the option of functioning on a case-by-case basis or for specific tasks. This can still be beneficial for a start-up artist by providing prestige, showing the industry a credible manager is behind the artist, making them take the artist more seriously. In this way a manager may reveal their involvement more officially to awaken the interest of labels etc after the artist has laid the setting. Also, if the manager is known to be skillful in their work, the industry should assume that this expertise has been used to benefit the artist's affairs and position.

If it is already clear the job will be done on a day-to-day basis, a few specific conditions should be noted. Tune into 'artist first' thinking. Personal issues shouldn't prevent successful manager performance. Remember, each manager has their own working style, so needs are individual. It is not in anyone's interest if motivation runs out at the very beginning. No-one will take over if it isn't worth it.

The most important thing to a manager is usually their commission, the reward. It enables working peace to get an artist's career running. Usually commission is settled somewhere close to 20 percent of the artist's income – when acting as a day-to-day manager. For case-by-case tasks, a fixed fee could be practical so as not to eat any equities from the artist's side. Percentage may also vary between different income types for example from recording royalties a manager receives 15 percent while advertising agreements provides 25. It depends what parties feel is appropriate.

There are of course bigger and lower percentages in use, but this is the median. There are many things affecting rate. Pay attention to the base from which commission will be calculated. Is it from artist revenue as a gross earning, or the artist's net income. Percentages are usually lower if artist revenue is used for the calculation. If commission is calculated from the net, anything that causes costs also lowers commission. From the manager's perspective, it might be beneficial to seek clarifications and preconditions in this regard. For example, as the artist increases their costs in their operations, not all of these are counted as factors that reduce the commission.

Time frames for the manager's commission right should also be determined. In some agreements, the manager's commission applies only to musical works released during the term, excluding all else. It is a question of what's fair. Many things affect this, with no single solution.

The costs associated with the assignment should also be thought upon. Managers shouldn't be responsible for costs when running management. The artist is the owner of copyright and thus it's only fair they are liable for costs. The manager's commission is reflective of this. Nothing states that this cannot occur, however. A manager may run things at their own cost. If this is the case, reimbursements are strictly stated in the agreement.

No matter the reimbursement system agreed upon, details need to be explicitly described, limiting management costs per month, or requiring prior approval.

As already discussed, also pay attention to post-termination conditions.

A manager agreement establishes exclusivity, but usually applies only to the artist. Due to uncertainty and other practicalities however, a manager reserves the right to render similar services to other artists and usually rules out 24/7 devotion. A manager is available when reasonably expected, but initial projects and early stage careers sometimes require more effort on this part. The sooner things get running, the faster commission mechanisms work. Strictly following contract rules is not always necessary – it is more of a guideline.

4.6.4. The Assignment

An assignment itself usually consists of three main concepts – management itself, professional guidance and intermediation. It is important to decide how far representation extends – music business only, or the entire entertainment industry.

To assess your own contribution in this and the meaningfulness of the task, transfer the artist's current situation onto that transparent wall and see how the artist appears through the eyes of different audiences. Then evaluate what should be done next. Afterward, contemplate what you can do yourself and how willing you are to do it. By following this process, you'll gain clarity on the options and whether you are the right person for the task.

For a manager, it is crucial to accept the fact you may need to go the extra mile, even beyond contractual obligations, to accomplish a mission. It takes time to get things running and is important sufficient resources are reserved. It is also advisable an artist takes note of this. For reimbursements clauses where an artist is responsible for costs, it is common courtesy to provide an estimate in order to prepare.

Management nowadays is usually a co-management system between the artist and manager. It is not uncommon for the artist to be responsible for overall strategy and the manager is the executing party. If an artist has no manager then management is handled themselves. The division of labor is important in any case.

A manager can be set as the responsible for overall strategy due to their expertise and knowledge. The artist is then prepped and updated with the current agenda. For example the manager would design the functional parts of an artist's online posts or communication with audiences and the artist then includes ingredients meaningful to them.

The emphasis should be on the word resources, with both the manager and artist having their own. In an ideal situation, each task is performed by the member with the resources to complete it for the common goal. If a band member is a genius with computers, it would be natural that he or she is the one in charge of building the website, for example.

This is the initial setting – the beginning of everything. When things progress the set-up can be changed. An artist may no longer have time to take part in management. Resources and willingness to use them will determine how to proceed. If a manager's position is economically sound, he or she can start to focus on other things when there is no longer a need to struggle with resource acquisition. A manager may naturally become more responsible for management and maybe even require an assistant.

Settings may change for reasons other than economical. This is a circumstantial relationship where necessity determines what to do next. For example, if a group member becomes occupied, the organizational line-up requires changes, or an artist's success rapidly increases requiring extra resources.

The manager agreement itself shouldn't prevent progress – especially with regard to assignments. Changes are likely. A well-drafted agreement is one that lives and breathes throughout. When a part becomes obsolete, it is possible it may become needed again, thus the whole agreement need not be changed. Extra work from the manager will be compensated via commission or reimbursement through the agreement and there are terms put in place to deal with something unexpected. This allows a manager to estimate their moves without hesitation. Some things require fast reactions or may result in a lost opportunity.

Despite all the variables above, a manager is usually acquired for providing professional guidance, a supervisor and to act as a negotiator on the artist's behalf. A manager needs assess their own true possibility of managing a mission. If there are discrepancies, they need to be settled prior.

For an artist, it is essential to keep in mind how much and how long external support is needed. It is also relevant why. There's no point keeping a manager unless there's a true need, or you are just wasting each other's time and resources. A great relationship between a manager and artist develops along the way and is often evident in post-termination clauses. The longer a relationship continues, the longer the post-termination rights.

In modern music business, technology continuously creates new earning opportunities and it can be tempting to try every new avenue. It is the manager's task to maintain course and determine which avenues are worth undertaking – not every new trendy adventure needs to be accomplished.

This can be exhausting and requires constant monitoring. A great manager agreement considers a manager's challenges and makes the assignment meaningful, without which failure is usually inevitable.

5. COPYRIGHT

5.1. Observations

Now that we have seen one side of the coin, contracts, we can take the other side into consideration. Contracts cannot be without copyright, with almost every music business agreement somehow related to copyright. An artist is the only one who can act alone. An artist can be an artist without a recording company, but a recording company is nothing without an artist. If a manager has no artist to represent, there is nothing to manage, thus the artist is everything.

Let's recall the starting point, copyright is the ultimate trading good of this sector and initially belongs to the artist. It gives its owner exclusive rights to decide whether to exploit the work or not. One never has to publish it or provide permission for a release. It is completely up to the copyright holder what to do with it.

A copyright holder may give up rights only to parts of a song, such as the head riff. The main rule is explicit consent from its creator is required to exploit any part of a song.

Copyright does not require registration in order to obtain protection. You get copyright to work at the time of its creation. There are no quality requirements and it doesn't need to be an artistic masterpiece in order to acquire copyright protection. From this perspective, all copyrights are equal. Of course, if you ever want to gain economic benefits from it such as royalties, registration and attaching yourself into the relevant music recognition mechanisms are usually needed, otherwise users cannot track copyright payments.

Copyright protection lasts the life of the author plus an additional 70 years, with possible national differences and also with different types of copyright. However, the idea is clear – copyright has a far-reaching legal effect for its owner, making it desired merchandise. Competition legislature does not apply to it, with only a few exceptions to the main rule that you can apply it almost to whatever you want.

Today, it is increasingly common for works to have multiple creators that own the work together. Permission must therefore be obtained from all of them. An exception to this is where the parts are independent and distinguishable. If one has created the lyrics and the other the composition, they each own their part. If you only want to use the lyrics without the composition, then you only need permission from the lyricist.

Think of a song with multiple writers; this is where the previously mentioned sync placement scenarios come into play. Imagine a music supervisor who finds the desired song and notices that it has 12 rights owners. To clear the song for use in a specific scene of a movie, the supervisor would need to negotiate 12 contracts with these songwriters or their representatives. From a strategic perspective, such a scenario can be highly significant, especially if a competing song has only two rights holders, for example.

From an internal perspective, the situation requires a clear member agreement in the case of bands, to avoid disputes and discrepancies. If two or more songwriters write songs together, a co-writing agreement is necessary. The most common hurdle in exploiting copyright is situations where all necessary rights cannot be obtained and is why it is so important to first settle internal protocols.

5.2. Member Agreement

Member agreement is an essential agreement in which each member of a band sets their own conditions for the use of their contribution in the band's operations. If these issues are not agreed, one member may potentially veto and prevent some important measure in the band's operations. This can be particularly annoying if the contribution is not even significant, but still has the same inhibitory effect. Although this is rare, it is important for understanding copyright or publicity rights. Hence, the purpose of this agreement is to obtain each member's prior approval for cases like these.

With regard to copyright, members usually agree on split sheets. These can be done on a song-by-song, or recording-by-recording basis, but some bands find it sensible to have a predetermined protocol. A split sheet is a document that lists all respective song-writers of a song and also includes provisions on how financial shares will be arranged – who will get what. From a technical perspective, a split sheet is used to document the songwriter and composer information for the story root, indicating who should be attributed. The same applies to recordings.

Some member agreements may include priority presentation, where a member creates for example a riff and reveals it to the band, who then have maybe three weeks to decide whether to use it in the band's production. If they don't, the original creating member can use it freely. Although this is an extreme condition, it describes the very nature of copyright. When these initial settings clear, the next step is release or publication, depending on context, and new legal effects.

A release is the event where a **recording** is made available to the public for the first time, either physically or digitally. Publication is the moment a **song** is first revealed to the public. It is possible for an artist to release a published song as a cover song, leading to a single song having multiple recordings.

It is essential to know publication of a song does not necessarily require it to be recorded. It is enough that someone performs it live for the first time – along with required permission. Think of a new musical, for which repertoire has been composed. When this musical is released for the first time, we can say that its music is also published. A song is considered published if it meets certain registration criteria. This can be multi-complex and I'll try to maintain simplicity, with enough background relevant for understanding the matter.

Since we are discussing a member agreement, we will use a band as an example instead of an individual artist. Usually the first public appearance of a song takes place by a band. Most bands prefer to release first with a recording and afterwards use it in live performances or for livestreaming purposes. Because of this it is best to use the term release – the song connected with the band's recording. Not that the word publication wouldn't be equally important. Each released recording is publication of a song if it happens for the first time. If you release a cover song, you will release a recording from an already published song. A few words about music publishing and related song-writing is warranted.

5.2.1. Co-Writing Rights

First, you cannot release an unpublished song without the permission of its authors. If permission is obtained, a recording can be released and the related legal effects start to occur.

It is assumed each songwriter of the band has joined the appropriate performing rights organizations and copyright management organization(s). For more detailed information about copyright organizations, see for example Songtrust. Or from the performing rights side, ASCAP or BMI. These are excellent sources of updated information and they also regularly arrange free webinars. We are discussing here copyrights insofar as they apply to the theme of the book. This will save on pages in this book.

The song writing essentials relevant to music business management and member agreement involve submitting a notification of a piece of work to a copyright organization. Once registered, you give up some administrative rights, allowing anyone to make a recording of it or play it live, given that the required licenses are obtained, or notifications of its use. This is nothing to be afraid of as it provides benefits through tracking the use of your songs, agreeing on licenses for its use and also collecting royalties on your behalf. This can in turn increase your income by avoiding the tedious task of each use requiring case-by-case interactions, which could turn some potential users away.

The heart of the collective administration and most typical situations where song-writers earn these royalties are when their songs are streamed on Spotify and other digital service providers, broadcasted on radio/TV, or performed live. Please note that there are certain restrictions on the usage of your music. Copyright organizations are unable to grant permission for the incorporation of your music in sheet or game music, as well as its inclusion in TV commercials, movies, TV series, or other audiovisual materials. Collective administration covers audio use only. These uses, which fall outside collective administration, open up the opportunity for artists to determine pricing freely.

A Hollywood blockbuster may generate a substantial amount of money, if you can get your music included in it. However, you may grant permission with next to no compensation if the association provides some other benefit or objective you don't want to miss.

Keep in mind a collective administration does not cover the alteration of songs. Translations, parts or a particular riff of a song requires a license and can only be obtained directly from songwriters, or respective music publishers. This involves another industrial body – the music publisher.

The words music publishing can be misleading. It's not really about publishing, but administration and song management. The term probably dates back to days where sheet music was needed to perform music. Performing artists needed a repertoire and found the best way was in sheet music. As already mentioned, music publishing also has its own concept of ownership. Even though songwriters would get a bigger economic share as the publisher, they usually sign away administration rights and control, leaving the publisher to decide on exploitation.

Copyright organizations are the primary administrators for audio use and music publisher administers all the other rights. Music publishers also manage synchronization rights, sheet music and rights to alter songs, most often with exclusive rights. They obtain this through a music publishing agreement with the songwriter and as a result, the music publisher gets the publisher's share of song revenue and administrative rights for song management. Remember, if an artist doesn't have a music publisher, the artist themself is their music's publisher.

The publisher's share is not limited only to administration rights, but also includes collective rights. After a music publishing agreement is signed, a letter of direction to each copyright organization administering the songwriter's songs will automatically determine allocation of song contributions.

Not all songwriters have a publishing agreement or want a publisher, instead they are the publisher. If this is the case, a few things should be considered. In the US, you cannot get mechanical royalties unless you are a publisher, which requires establishing your own publishing company – a massive operation just to set up let alone to run. Collective management organizations, such as Songtrust make things easier via their mutual agreements and arrangements for mechanical royalty collection with many copyright organizations and digital service providers around the world. Against a fee, they administer and collect the money you are owed, allowing you to keep your copyright compared to music publishing agreements. The Mechanical Licensing Collective, The MLC, also serves this same purpose.

Music publishers also provide creative services, such as active searches for new placements of a song, co-writing or facilitating working conditions, or providing advances. It is circumstantial whether a songwriter chooses to have a publisher. As we have many times addressed, every artist has their own individual needs, goals and resources.

Concerning Songtrust, they don't offer creative services or pitching support, but they may assist you if you have independently obtained an agreement (such as a sync agreement) and need support in managing it. In other words, while a music publisher actively seeks new avenues for your music, with Songtrust, those responsibilities fall on your shoulders.

Co-writing parts are especially important. Consider a far-fetched example where some band members haven't joined any copyright organizations. Every time explicit approval must be acquired from them for use of a song they were involved in, or at least power-of-attorney authentication. Such examples are rare, but these things need to be in place in advance. The easiest way is if all members give permission for the split sheet submitted to collective management organizations, or one member is in charge of the songs, but again, this is individual.

Similarly to other aspects of the music business, music publishing contracts have their tactical side. That is, additional value is sought through the contract or if there's another reason for it. One important aspect to investigate is what a music publisher actually does for your catalog and how well they are positioned in the industry. Do they receive information about upcoming sync placements, the needs of recording artists and can they influence them? Secondly, has the publisher organized their own organization in a way that makes them eligible to receive mechanical royalties.

If these conditions are not met to a satisfactory extent, a music publishing contract becomes a document through which you'll be transferring 25–50 percent of performance and mechanical royalties to the music publisher without a reasonable cause. So, be diligent in this regard.

5.2.2. Recording Rights

Member agreement copyright also applies to recordings. Each member's contribution should end up in recordings or they are not entitled to any recording royalties, streaming payouts, or performance royalties that, for example, radio play may generate. This is important to consider in line-up changes.

If a new guitarist becomes part of a band, future releases are relevant – the more, the greater the share. The nature and persistence of copyright and related rights applies to the former guitarist, as long as prior recordings exist in use, royalties and other copyrights are compensated to him or her. Copyright isn't related to band membership, but actual contributions, which is one manifestation of how copyright enables passive income. It is important to have clear statements for co-writing and recording situations.

For example, let's say you are that former guitarist. You were part of the band for the first three successful albums. If your involvement has been structured correctly, you are entitled to royalties for the entire legal protection period, even if you are no longer part of the band.

5.2.3. Publicity Rights

The member agreement also involves publicity rights – your name, image or likeness. Also, voice. One notable topic in the making of this book is vocal clones. They might potentially become a significant aspect of business in the future. No one can use them without your permission. Even if this appears to be self-evident, it is good to agree on this – especially in relation to third-party arrangements. A member agreement could ensure each member gives prior consent for their name, image and likeness to be used to achieve a common objective, avoiding individual members preventing important agreements or something.

Members can apply individual and conditional terms on the use of their publicity rights and should be attached to the contract. This is a good place to raise moral rights. These can be seen as personal rights. There are two – the right to attribution means an artist has the right to protect their reputation by requiring their name be correctly mentioned when their output and person is used. The same also applies to co-writing rights and recording rights. The other moral right is the right to integration, meaning an artist can object to use they see harmful to their name and reputation as an artist. This can be anything and sometimes is difficult to determine. The inclusion of publicity rights is correctly stated in the contract if the conditions for granting them include the moral rights as implied terms.

Moral rights have significant economic importance in today's world. When you are associated as a contributor to a production, it becomes one of the most valuable assets of your social media capital. Your digital identity takes shape around them through the story root.

Artists' copyrights also have a defining function, automatically triggered by releasing music. Such an inherent attribute, without any separate connections, speaks volumes about its power and significance. Even if the music itself doesn't yet hold economic value, its mere existence does.

Manifestations of moral rights, such as the right to attribution, form the foundation of credits – an original right belonging to the author. Unlike economic rights, moral rights cannot be entirely waived. Therefore, even if you have sold all your rights to a production, you are still credited as its author.

Moreover, the concept of a story root presented in this book would be rather feeble without including the author. Additionally, an artist doesn't necessarily have to use their real name; they can publish under a pseudonym or anonymously.

Before approving any of these aforementioned rights, you should really take a deeper look at what you really want. Consider exclusions related to co-writing and recording rights and make sure they are taken care of. This in itself, is a good reason to use member agreements. This will evaluate your true motivation and interests.

Management has partial responsibility to ensure copyrights etc are in order before going forward. If the management of the artist's copyrights is not handled properly, all parties involved may miss out on their respective shares. Each member's position should be in line with their efforts – both artistically and economically. After internal protocol is established, it is time to look outside.

5.3. Granting of Rights

As already mentioned, a record company cannot exist without an artist, but before they can work with an artist they must obtain certain rights from the artist. The same applies to other music industry arrangements – permission from the artist is required.

Before more closely examining granting of rights, we must break down the economic rights originally belonging to the artist. There are six. In order to obtain enabling licenses for economic exploitation, the company must usually obtain explicit power for most of them, by signing a recording agreement or a licensing agreement. In a licensing agreement, the artist retains ownership, while in a recording agreement, the artist forfeits all or some rights to the label.

The artist holds the power and right to
– perform the work publicly
– reproduce the work
– distribute the work
– make a derivative of the work

– display the work to the public

– prevent the recording from being streamed

Of these exclusive rights or controls are easy to perceive and some require definition, resulting in some lengthy recording agreements. But all manner of possibilities are important to include – consider an older agreement not including future technologies within the scope of an agreement, resulting in a company not having rights to reproduce a recording, or release or distribute it. Economic losses can be substantial, especially if the new technology becomes a primary method for consuming music.

Reproduction rights are at the core of a recording agreement. A label's main objective is not just for physical ownership of a master recording, but the content too, so they can exploit it to the fullest potential.

In line with the theme of this book, music business management, it is essential to consider what is reasonable to sign away. Today, it is increasingly common for artists to limit granting of rights, considering their contribution so valuable they usually only give up partial ownership of it. Artist management should aim for this in negotiations, to ensure a better position for the artist than if the label would own the master.

Despite these ideals, remember the motivations of all parties involved. If your contractual partner does not feel satisfied with their part, it may affect their attitude. This may not necessarily be a good thing, even if the contract is favorable to you in terms of its content. In management, you always need to look at the bigger picture.

Time limited ownership is another option, where after for example 10 years, ownership would return to the artist. For the estimated active period the partner gives added value to your endeavors. This ensures an artist's partners are actively working for them. When the partnership ends, so do the rights. Be mindful of post-termination considerations in this scenario however, as some rights remain in force by law – even if an agreement expires.

Be aware that co-writing rights are not part of a recording agreement, they are part of music publishing agreements. Recording rights belong in recording agreements and it's important not to overstep the bounds of a contract.

A label will likely need permission for publicity rights to adequately market and promote according to the demands of a recording agreement. Sometimes you need a separate agreement specifying this, when publicity rights are, for example, to be used out of the traditional scope of a recording agreement. This kind of clarification is needed when the label, for example, obtains the right to issue NFT's on behalf of the artist. Expanded rights out of the traditional scope of an agreement should naturally be agreed in a separate agreement. This way, if some part of the whole fails, it does not ruin an existing partnership.

However, don't be alarmed if you find such terms in a recording contract. It's not as categorically wrong as mixing the terms of a music publishing agreement and a recording contract. A skilled contract drafter with sufficient legal knowledge can write NFT-related sections into the recording contract in a way that eliminates the aforementioned risk.

This is also an area where in the future there will be considerations regarding voice clones. If the record label obtains usage and exploitation rights for them, this is where the terms for compensating the artist will be negotiated.

Also, whenever you are granting rights to any copyrights and/or related rights, you shouldn't grant more than necessary.

The wording of an agreement also shouldn't entice anyone to interpret the agreement more broadly than originally intended.

Finally, one of the six rights mentioned earlier deserves further clarification – the right to display music. This is entirely related to different situations than where music is used. Typically, a painting is put on display. However, there are two types of displays for an artist. You can put the artist's sheet music and lyrics on display – for example, on LyricFind or even having excerpts manufactured onto mugs. Each of these inclusions can be a significant business opportunity. You never know when a catchy chorus from a song becomes a big hit on the side of a mug.

5.3.1. Sync Agreement

A synchronization agreement is similar to a recording agreement in many respects. Initially, the license must be obtained from all members of a band that took part in the recording. A new member that wasn't involved in the recording is not required to give consent, however the former member must give permission.

Synchronization licenses cannot be obtained from collective management organizations, instead directly from the rights-owners. Note that a synchronization license must be acquired separately for both the **recording and composition**, it isn't sufficient to just get a license for the recording.

We are not talking about the score, that is music composed and recorded especially for a film that is designed to fit a story and its scenes and often adheres to a strict timecode. We are referring to recordings an artist already has done or will record in the future. For example, each new James Bond movie usually chooses an artist to write a theme song for it.

Here we return to the very essence of a recording agreement – master recording ownership. The owner of the master recording has the power to grant these licenses on behalf of all other rights owners and recording artists. These should be considered in advance, especially if the master recording is jointly owned or an artist acts independently. This is also where an independent artist's homepage should contain instructions for these inquiries and who to contact.

The same is true for compositions of a particular recording where you need to obtain a license for its use from the rights owners. Member agreements will manage this and if a band has signed a music publishing agreement, the license must be acquired from the music publisher. If there is no music publisher, the license must be obtained from each member, individually, unless a power-of-attorney is in place for one member to agree on the license. However, you can never be certain when it comes to copyright, so it would still be wise to get approval from each and every writer to make sure there is no ambiguity.

For artists whose music is written by someone else, it can be tricky – the licensing party isn't necessarily the same body and the song may have seven writers, some of which have a music publisher and some not. In this case, all permissions are required in order to obtain a license for use.

A synchronization agreement differs from a recording agreement via a few important details. Even though the granting of rights is pretty much similar to a recording agreement, a sync agreement is non-exclusive – meaning the license is only for a specific film or synchronization purpose. Validity is usually timeless. It would be difficult to exploit a movie, with uncertainty whether the music is valid for the life of the movie's copyright. Even if such a right were perpetual, the underlying license may be subject to renewal at certain intervals, and additional conditions may be imposed on the right. So, it's more of a starting point.

In the same way a recording company's right to use an artist's publicity rights can only be in relation to marketing purposes – a synchronization license can only be attached to the film and its marketing. If a wider scope is desired, an additional agreement is required, such as for an original soundtrack from the movie.

One more note on sync agreements to wrap up. You have the power to determine the price at which you grant such consent. If it's a big-budget studio-produced movie expected to be a blockbuster, the sync fee can likely be higher. It also depends on the film's budget, how much they've allocated for the music and how much of that budget is already spent or available. Additionally, you will receive royalties for performance rights when the film is shown on television or in other similar contexts in the future. So, you can never predict this accurately. A low-budget indie film where you don't receive a substantial upfront fee may surprise everyone by being shown in hundreds of countries multiple times. Therefore, even if the original sync fee was modest, the associated performance royalties can be significant. An up-to-date management should already be considering various pricing strategies for different situations, as each sync placement is unique. Furthermore, if such an inquiry ever arises, it often requires a quick response.

Another pricing-related aspect is the MFN (Most Favored Nations) clause. This means that if $5000 is paid for the recording's sync fee, the composition should also receive the same amount.

5.3.2. Music Publishing Agreement

Music publishing can come in all sorts of interesting configurations. It is completely possible members have different publishers. Perhaps originally only one member was meant to be the songwriter and over time, other members also take part in song writing. Just a reminder because this is so important, and it's an ongoing matter that needs attention, not only for artists but also for managers. A music publishing agreement may appear somewhat innocuous on paper, but it may contain far-reaching restrictions that could significantly diminish an artist's position, even far into the future. Hence, if you're using these rights as bargaining chips to achieve something else valuable, make sure it's worth it. It is imperative to agree on control for jointly owned music.

Ownership and control does not always run parallel. Even with a greater share of song revenue, you may still lose control of the work, which is usually the case with music publishing agreements where the publisher gets the administrative right and related control. If you do not agree with this, especially with regard to moral rights, you shouldn't sign a music publishing agreement. If there is no other choice, the agreement should at least contain restrictions to the publisher's control so some explicit uses are ruled out of the scope.

The great thing about copyright is that the author is free to decide whether to take money for its use or not. You may call this artistic freedom. The ultimate power of a copyright holder. This power is evident in situations where the work, either a song or recording, is currently unpublished or not yet released. This can be withheld for whatever reason. A member agreement reaching a common goal such as the band's overall welfare, may find you forfeiting your rights for something greater. Not always advisable, but in some cases wise. If you are mainly a composer, your reputation is at stake. A band may give permission for a sync placement without any reward, if conditions are beneficial in other ways. On the other hand, an individual movie composer has the threat that their music will not be taken seriously and it would not reflect well in the industry if it is seen that their music is cheap.

This is also a bridge to intermediation – our next chapter. The business in music is made with arrangements where an artist's writing, recording and publicity rights are exploited and should always be the starting point. The other side is about story enrichment with its business-related elements, but before you reach these you need resources. Usually resources come first, then profit and this is where intermediation comes in.

6. INTERMEDIATION

6.1. The Concept

Intermediation used to be the most visible feature of artist management. Many people still think a great manager is behind an artist getting recording agreements, featuring in a game-changing interview or getting sync placement, through people knowing people. This may partly still be true, but not in the way as before. The independent sector is constantly growing and increasing its significance. Artists are increasingly operating with their own teams. They may not necessarily need record labels to succeed in their endeavors.

A recording company used to be what facilitated an artist's success in their early days – without them you couldn't even dream about success. The artist wasn't taken seriously before the recording contract and their career took off professionally with that agreement. That is, industry approval was required. Labels were what made music available to the public – through vinyl, cassette or CD. Nowadays all that is required is an upload to Spotify and/or other DSP's. A label was required to carry out distribution, as well as actual promotion and so an artist's career started with a recording agreement. No wonder it was management's main target.

The artist's main job was to have a song or other musical talent with hit potential. The manager as the connecting factor, facilitated as favorable as possible circumstances for the artist and negotiated agreements. The same is also true today, but slightly differently. It's still about great songs, great performers or some other talent, but usually requires an additional boost from the artist. To get a recording agreement you usually require social media following and/or fan engagement – and this is before serious negotiations even start. While it isn't necessarily so black and white – an artist may still begin their career with a recording agreement (that's what marketing departments are for) – current trends reflects this.

It is recommended to connect with the label a&r's during a strategically timely moment. This used to be when an artist had something exceptional to present in terms of music, today we wait for when an artist's online presence has crossed the 'label threshold' and thus the artist's online presence, story root and related episodes attract in a meaningful way. And behind this, there's still a story and/or business to enrich. This requires a whole different set of qualities from management. Recording agreements more often reflect the time is right to work together, not necessarily the result of negotiation. Facilitating negotiations are still necessary, but for slightly different reasons. Manager facilitation also enhances future prospects for an artist through a label becoming aware of their existence.

At this point, we could bring up industry tracking. There are two types of tracking that are relevant to an artist, human-driven and machine-driven. When you consciously set out to make an artist interesting, you need to consider this division and each of them requires action. It's entirely different to include information for AI's needs compared to what the industry would want to know about the artist. In general, the artist's online presence should align with the goals you're aiming to achieve through these intermediations. If the artist aims to impress a potential record label, their online presence must be such that the label's interest increases rather than decreases. Or if the artist wants AI to understand something about them, it needs to be fed in such a way that the information is registered. The artist should become recognized in a way that highlights their inherent appeal.

Intermediation is used to convince someone outside your own organization and there are usually many ways to make that happen. It's not uncommon to spend a long time circling around a certain issue and the relevant industrial bodies and individuals before you find a compelling reason to make initial contact. Or how to present a particular matter to a party you're familiar with. This, in turn, requires continuous monitoring and research from the manager. When that punch line finally opens up, everything usually flows more naturally.

To establish or run a business requires intermediation activity to get what's needed, but remember this may take time to map out all the possibilities and find the right partners. Sometimes this phase is seamless without distractions and other times may take years to establish. A manager has to consider this and be prepared to work beyond contractual obligations in order to get things started.

It is important to distinguish between *within* industry and *for* industry. Intermediation within industry relates to acquiring resources important to progress such as getting a recording agreement. Intermediation for industry likely deals with additional revenue. Passive promotion goes hand in hand with active promotion. When passive promotion is set up to support these intermediation efforts, you'll expose yourself and your operation to suggestions that you might not have taken into account. Passive promotion has significant power, so a little word of caution is in order at this point.

Situations occasionally pop up where money is available to you quickly. But think deeply about what it would represent if you accept it. Would there be adverse effects on other vital operations? This could create very tricky situations and it is difficult to evaluate right from wrong, let alone reactions.

Consider being the manager of two or three artists, whose careers still require substantial work to become economically secure for both them and you. An offer comes in from an artist with better prospects. You've been struggling financially and now this is a chance to change things. Evaluate overall effects if you said yes. The money doesn't always count. Will your other artists suffer? Your working conditions and motivation? Think about the moral issues involved and your reputation. These kinds of deliberation are common for managers before agreeing to assignments. It is also courteous to inform others to prepare them of your intentions.

Intermediation isn't only for resource acquisition or business objectives, but is similarly important for an artist's story and promotion. Whilst an operation may intend to temporarily raise an artist's visibility, for example with a ground breaking interview, it may also come to support future goals without immediate effect – establishing a new chapter in the artist's online presence and related passive promotion. Keep this in mind when actively enriching a story and we will come back to consistency requirements.

Implementation of such an operation requires an external factor, the reporter, the core of an intermediation activity and how we make it happen. Before the interview is published, the artist is at the mercy of others, with many hurdles in between that will have to be taken into account. Intermediation operations consists of three inter-related phases – facilitation, implementation and output. Just like in many other management tasks, there is a technical and tactical aspect to this as well.

The technical side concerns the operation and its process. How to seamlessly make something happen – a meaningful interview, recording agreement negotiation or meeting with festival promoters. All these involve intermediary activity – although some are like a series of stepping stones to reach a goal. A one-on-one meeting with an artist could convince a festival promoter to consider them in a festival line-up, which is certainly worth trying.

The tactical side of intermediation is related to the impact it gathers, meaning all outputs that result in an effect through different areas of action. Good management can read between the lines and consider in advance the results of an accepted offer, also taking note the course of events. Things can be corrected if something offends others as the elimination of damages to reputation is also part of successful intermediation – mending insulted, upset or undervalued parties can work wonders for improving situations on both sides of a disagreement.

Like other music business features, intermediation also has a passive dimension. A side detail may be highlighted through a specific goal that causes a recipient to view things differently, which is the goal of passive promotion. As we strive for the important story-on-story effect, we may also give birth to meaningful business opportunities and potential follow-ups, even those we have not specifically aimed for.

It is usually the manager's job to filter through the ocean of opportunities, combining an artist's dreams and prospects and maintaining involvement through background actions, at the same time as matching short term goals with a long term agenda.

An artist meeting with a festival promoter may happen in the same room that a Fortnite representative is present and whilst showing the artist's excerpts from previous venues leads to a serendipitous occurrence that results in the artist being invited for talks to star in the Fortnite metaverse. You may not succeed with the festival slot, but end up performing in Fortnite's metaverse.

Sometimes facilitation is intentional, if management knows in advance a meeting has additional eyes and ears. Oftentimes it is about industry connections – the more the industry knows you, the better the prospects. Each and every encounter may have a potential outcome.

6.2. Consistency

Consistency should go hand in hand with every moment. Consider it an artist's biography where a good one tells the story chronologically, but also illuminates the background.

Discography can be used as the frame for consistency and is also the origin for the story root. With each release, single or entire album, another chapter is added to the artist's promotion and related storyline – likely with different meanings to different audiences. The most important one – the public, fans and super fans – should have their expectations matched for continuation from the previous release. An artist must do what feels best, but the wishes of fans is worth considering too.

Sometimes business motives conflict with story elements. An artist at the top of their popularity may exceed their story root and genre boundaries. Success may add temptation to artificially acquire additional turnover, but the end result may go too far from the original theme and may distract from future prospects.

Since intermediation is always about things that do not yet exist, its implementation should fit into frames of the artist's story, but also with expectations of the artist's audiences. Ideally, it should never incorporate elements that don't belong. Sometimes there are no other choices but to break these boundaries, such as an artist has ran out of resources and no other options exist. Smoothing and limiting the impact can help manage such situations, as well as in some cases explaining the reasoning to various audiences – sometimes publicly and sometimes privately, depending on the situation.

Never forget the true influence of your fans. If a deviation is explained well, their reaction can justify it to other audiences, resulting in similar reactions with the media, industry and among the digital realm. It is usually the task of management to correct such incidents.

Industry liaison involves a lot of uncertainties and is quite different from communication with fans. This is especially true when communicating online and not face to face. You may miss something important – an essential motive that isn't always obvious – especially if it is personal.

It is important to clear up issues or revisit conversations to ensure all avenues and collaborations come to fruition. Often situations are not spoken about and are ignored – or worse, a reputation is ruined by inaction. This can also happen in business terms – you may have inadvertently ignored another party's interest. An invitation to dance lies hidden behind some other expression. Being aware is the key to making things happen.

If you are on a record label's radar and they reach out, it doesn't always proceed with a simple response to an offer. The record label might easily initiate a conversation where they are testing you. If you can pick the fruits of the discussion and move it forward, you are likely to succeed in your operation.

Motives and interest fluctuate over time, especially if negotiations last a long time and become exhausting. This may require a calculated gradual release of motivating elements in order to succeed. You'll need to know where to start and when to start. Each collaboration has a sweet spot to take advantage of and make things happen, although unfortunately things don't always go the way we would expect.

One important point to make here is to ensure that your online presence's spirit aligns with the themes and claims you use in negotiations. Inconsistencies at that interface are easy to spot. This can also be a place where your credibility is tested. As mentioned earlier, inactivity – if your negotiating partner suddenly steps back, the reason could be here.

The situation is somewhat similar to contract negotiations. If the draft contract doesn't align with the discussions that took place, there are likely to be consequences. The reliability of the collaboration is evaluated throughout the process and it can fall apart right on the finishing line.

When trying to set up a collaboration you need to be certain of where you want things to go, but also initially be discrete. The recipient's time is at stake and you may have to dance around the subject to open lines of communication. Don't move too fast, but not too slow. A situation will determine what is next and it is possible you end up with a completely different outcome than originally planned. You must then decide whether it is acceptable. Usually the one with higher needs of a contract has the greater responsibility for ensuring smooth communication.

Remember it is very common to use middlemen – especially in the music business – and even by managers. It is easiest to send someone who knows the recipient to the first meeting, but you are ultimately responsible for your choices as a manager. If negotiations fail or have a complicated start, things need to be corrected, so it is always recommended to take the lead for the first few steps to make sure of a green light before delegating.

This is especially evident during recording agreement negotiations and as a manager you are expected to both prepare the artist regarding the contract and its obligations and also complete business arrangements for the artist to walk in to everything set up. This allows an artist to concentrate on their job without hesitation or uncertainties. We have already mentioned transparency and how things are better when an artist knows what has gone on behind the scenes, knowing what is expected of them and also what they can expect from the agreement.

Due to its artificial nature, intermediation carries its risks. It's especially important to understand why and when it's being practiced. Sometimes, it can become too routine, particularly during quieter times. You might not even realize that some preparatory work is in progress, even though the results are not yet visible. In such moments, you might hastily include material that has questionable relevance to the overall plan. This material constantly emerges, even in skilled management. Thus, the other side of intermediation, besides story enrichment, is to eradicate unnecessary actions and workstreams.

The negative residuals associate with intermediation. Sometimes, despite many efforts, a project doesn't succeed. You can't always disappear from the spotlight when this becomes evident. It may require damage control and proactive measures to maintain relationships and prevent unnecessary harm. Usually, the responsibility lies with the party who initiated the negotiations or who needs a certain agreement more.

6.3. Control

Intermediation takes place in a landscape not under complete control of an artist and you cannot dictate terms, unlike on your website.

When an operation requires the contribution of others it almost without exception brings variables and alternative motives, involving direct and indirect effects. Even if negotiations have gone well and a contract agreed, you should consider the wider effects as it's possible the end result doesn't head in the desired direction.

In principle there are two types of control – one associated with negotiations and their organization, and the other the negotiating result itself. Remember the negotiating result usually obliges you to act accordingly. A promised exclusive interview where you later decide to do an additional interview with another media outlet will have consequences. The first media outlet may refuse to cooperate with you in the future. Recording agreements are usually exclusive and parallel activities are prohibited within the sphere of its influence. When facilitating intermediation consider how the end result fits into existing plans and surrounding circumstances.

Control is also present during negotiations. Although you cannot really completely dictate the course, you can control its impact taking into account other areas of action. Only rarely negotiations are so important you can afford to completely stop other vital functions such as when industrial or other external expectations incite you to start something entirely new.

If an artist is popular in the United States, doing a tour there may take advantage of current industry, media and fan opinion, and should be acted on accordingly. Implementation of such an operation is always laborious and time-consuming, but the easiest solution would be to get the artist to piggyback to have the artist open for a popular headliner. This requires case-by-case consideration as a tour in this manner would not be the same as a solo tour. On one hand popularity cannot always be precisely known in a new geographical area and a solo tour may fail after much negotiation and planning. Resources and other areas of action are important to evaluate in such a situation to determine feasibility and sensibility of investing in such opportunities.

Probability and anticipation play a part and such may well be the next sensible step if there is nothing else pressing on the table. These may also create follow-ups which would not otherwise be possible.

Remember, when additional projects are in the planning stage, it's always necessary to be prepared to abandon them. Management should carefully map out potential reputation damage control. What if the tour doesn't happen after it has already been hinted at or even officially advertised. Exit plans are part of every operation. This is another reason to avoid success claims around unrealized matters.

From a technical point of view, control is present at the point where negotiations start until the moment where the agreement itself is signed. That is, when you have made your decision to start something new and it requires external resources, the only thing you have to do is its technical implementation. It is essential to evaluate all the things that can go wrong and move on in a way circumstances require, which may require advance steps. There are many great guides written on how to run negotiations smoothly or how to approach recipients in an effective way, but you will find your own way. Some managers steer actions to avoid self-initiated negotiations, instead inviting attention through great performances elsewhere, for example online presence optimization, making labels and other industrial bodies approach them.

6.4. Artist's Control

We have dealt with control from the outside, now we will talk about how it looks inside the artist's organization and to the question of the artist and manager's relationship. Even though an artist is ultimately in charge of operations and the owner of copyright, the manager may take the lead from time to time. This is usually because prevailing circumstances are not favorable for the artist's goal, story or a meaningful plan, or the artist is completely unaware of these needs. The manager has been assigned due to their field knowledge or other capacity and may suggest additional moves with the agreement between them deciding how these steps will be taken.

There are usually parallel motives behind such an action. Sometimes emphasis is on the artist's needs and sometimes the manager's, but usually it's for both and quite possibly a mandatory function. The exact reasoning is unimportant, as long as these functions are seamlessly embedded in the current situation, with consideration to reluctance and enjoyment of particular operations.

Additional activities are required usually to ease economic strain and bring in resources in order to carry out the artist's plan. A balance between industrial expectations and the artist's view needs to occur. Sometimes the only way to achieve this is through a separate story line. Involving fans in the operation is another approach that brings additional motivation and is always highly appreciated. Costs, both financial and emotional or reputational need to be considered in such situations, as well as the attention that each new endeavor may require. The important outcome is the feeling of everyone involved – fans, the artist and management – and justification of the project's incorporation into the story. In some cases resource acquisition is organized for other reasons, such as increasing a manager's resources. Performing a crucial operation may require additional funds or other resources. If the manager is the one executing it, the necessary resources must be allocated for it.

Difficult times should be thought of as opportunities to create something new, and hence, additional episodes for an artist's story. The exquisite feature of intermediation is that it can happen everywhere. The main question is how much first-hand decision-making power the manager should have.

In general, the relationship between artist and manager is a growth story – a good relationship is one that breaths well in ever-changing situations. It must still be ensured that the artist always has the final say.

One manifestation of the modern music business is to own your own promotion. This is good to remember when practicing intermediation. Each measure aims at enhancing an artist's reach. Among the public, an artist hopes for fans. Among the media, an artist wishes for recognization and visibility. Among industry, an artist wants to be a recognized professional with unrestricted access to resources, or at least negotiating opportunities. In the digital realm, an artist aims to have a presence that aligns with and supports their strategic objectives. The artist can influence opportunities and for this purpose there is anticipation, a skill that develops along the way. Before that, one contemporary perspective where the various faces of intermediation come into play.

6.5. A Music Supervision Point of View

6.5.1. Music Supervision Through The Management's Scope

Allow me to offer a uniqueness to this book. Music supervision entails so many aspects that need consideration in everyday management, presented in a more condensed form compared to comprehensive music publishing or recording contracts.

In the context, there are similar elements of rights licensing as in those agreements, and at the same time, it involves an intermediation process. Success in the task requires the involvement of music supervisors. As managers, we can proceed in various ways and utilize combinations of these methods. We can try to build relationships within the music supervision community ourselves or seek a suitable sync agent to take care of this task for us. If neither of these seems appealing, we can direct the artist towards music libraries, where many music supervisors search for music for their productions.

In this regard, music supervision forms a suitable reflective surface for the theme of this book. Against this backdrop, we can present several conceptual models and apply them into practice.

Here are a few observations related to the book. When discussing music supervision, our initial managerial task is to identify the situation. The music supervisor is the entity responsible for selecting music for audiovisual productions and acquiring the rights to it. Therefore, to succeed in this task, we need their cooperation. This means that we should be aware of how they perceive all of this – it greatly impacts our success in our own endeavors.

Music supervision is an excellent example of a managerial task as it's an optimally defined entity that nevertheless touches upon all three compartments of management. Therefore, we need to consider various influences when carrying out this task. Securing a significant sync placement for our artist will likely have a broader impact on the artist's promotion. It is very possible that such an agreement could become a turning point in the entire career.

Similarly to other management tasks, technical and tactical requirements also apply here. The technical requirements are related to how the music should be delivered to supervisors and scene-specific criteria. If a particular scene requires music of a specific tempo or to convey a certain mood, including vastly different types of music in the package might not be advisable.

Copyright is another technical requirement for sync placement. Without the consent of all the rights holders, this action cannot be executed. Since many music supervisors work on tight schedules, enabling the acquisition of rights quickly and effortlessly is advisable. Bringing this openly to the forefront is likely to enhance your chances. Perhaps you're interested in familiarizing yourself with the use of Soundcloud or DISCO. These platforms facilitate various activities and transactions related to music supervision.

The tactical side, on the other hand, relates to the music supervisor's personality, preferences, and work history. Conducting your own research is always worthwhile. For instance, from the IMDb database, you can discover the types of productions they've been involved in and in what capacity. If there's a discernible pattern, you can utilize that in your communications. In the music business, there's a courteous tracking culture where the recipient is respected by understanding their backgrounds.

6.5.2. Contemplation

As a manager immersed in the world of music supervision, each interaction with music supervisors requires careful consideration and strategic approaches. Here are a few things to consider. These same guidelines apply to other tasks in the field that require intermediation.

Approaching Music Supervisors for Sync Placements: When initiating contact for sync placements, your approach need to take into consideration crafting a concise yet compelling introduction, showcasing the artist's uniqueness without overwhelming the supervisor. It's crucial to tailor the approach to fit the supervisor's preferences and workload, aiming for a balanced and respectful communication style.

Post-Contact Procedures: Once the initial connection is established, your focus shifts to nurturing this relationship. This involves timely follow-ups that express genuine interest in the supervisor's work, while also sharing relevant updates about the artist's creations. Building a rapport gradually, without being overly persistent, can be pivotal.

Communication Frequency and Etiquette: Balancing communication frequency can be a delicate task. The aim is to maintain a respectful distance while staying on their radar. It's about finding the sweet spot – not too infrequent to be forgotten, yet not too frequent to be deemed intrusive. Every touchpoint aims to add value or provide relevant updates.

Methods for Music Submission and Copyright Inclusion: Regarding music submissions, tailor each package meticulously, ensuring it's easily accessible and contains all necessary copyright information. The goal is to make the supervisor's job as effortless as possible while highlighting the artist's authenticity and appeal.

Artist Website Optimization: The artist's website serves as a dynamic portfolio for supervisors. Ensuring it includes concise yet comprehensive sync-related information, such as previous placements, enhances its appeal to music supervisors scouting for new sounds. You can also the add necessary instructions for acquiring rights there.

Timely Responses to Supervisor Interest: Promptness is key when responding to a supervisor's interest. It reflects the artist's professionalism and eagerness to collaborate. However, it's essential to balance speed with thoughtfulness, ensuring the response is well-crafted and aligned with the artist's brand.

Streamlining Rights Clearance: Proactively preparing rights clearance materials in advance ensures a seamless process. This involves staying updated on copyright and licensing requirements, preemptively addressing any potential hurdles.

Sync Placement Promotional Timing: Regarding promotional timing, seek clarity within the sync agreement regarding when announcements can be made. Align with industry norms, respecting the confidentiality of the project until the specified release parameters.

Challenges Faced by Music Supervisors: Understanding the challenges supervisors encounter allows us to tailor our approaches accordingly, fostering mutually beneficial relationships.

These contemplations guide our managerial decisions, shaping our interactions with music supervisors to maximize opportunities while respecting professional boundaries.

6.5.3. More Information

Naturally, there's so much more to this. If you want to learn more about the subject, a few music supervision courses and information sources deserve special mention.

From the music supervisor's perspective, Jennifer Pyken's Music Supervision Master Course, Trygge Toven's Sync Music Licensing Masterclass, or Ryan Svendsen's YouTube channel provide guidance on a subject that holds broader significance for successful management implementation.

Jennifer Pyken
https://www.musicsuper.net/courses/music-supervision-mastercourse

Trygge Toven
https://course.vidsyn.com

Ryan Svendsen
https://www.musicbefore.com

Eric Campbell's CTRL CAMP offers a slightly different perspective – these insights will be essential across the board in music business transactions.
https://ctrlcamp.com

Mac McIntosh's Musiclerk.com and The Sync Opps. on Patreon are also something to examine. In that Sync Opps, they regularly announce new and pending sync placement opportunities.
https://www.musiclerk.com
https://www.patreon.com/thesyncopps

Last but not least, DISCO's own School of Disco. It also provides a lot of information about the service itself. It's worth noting that these entities often visit each other's sets, bringing along various nuances in understanding matters.
https://www.disco.ac

If you want to get a comprehensive understanding of music supervision, it's advisable to explore all of these. This way, you'll gain slightly different perspectives. However, if you only have time or interest in one, each of these covers the subject sufficiently.

The lessons and insights gained from those sources can be applied analogously in other areas of the music business – especially when implementing intermediation. On the other hand, they have significant importance and impact on contracts and copyright. They reflect, in an understandable way, the specific traits of modern management in this field.

7. ANTICIPATION

7.1. Dimensions

Anticipation takes place in three different dimensions, within the compartments of management. For management this is a challenging task as all dimensions must be taken into account at the same time. Tasks need to be prepared in advance before they become relevant. The cost of anticipation in relation to benefit achieved should also be assessed.

Fixed costs, such as overheads and also unnecessary agreements should therefore be avoided when they have no grounds. A manager has to channel their own and joint resources in line with current income flow, but also plans and goals. These constantly fluctuate.

Some tasks' anticipation affect all compartments of management. Some tasks cause anticipation to focus only on the present project. A balance between the artist's objectives and how they fit into expectations of industry and other audiences is continually sought. Hence, the first two dimensions are related to operations and the third dimension is your own personal interest.

The third dimension, your own personal interest, requires the most premature action. You cannot proceed without personal security to some degree. This concerns all music business professions.

To approach this, you should try map out all your features with economic value. What is it that you intend to bring to the table. This will allow for easier decision making to accept agreements and give a better picture of what prior action is needed and whether to involve additional members. The paradox is that although artist management is a service profession, you must take care of yourself first. Field experience brings along expertise, enabling you to anticipate the actual workload of each task and better understand what success in the role truly requires.

7.2. Operations

Management tasks are influenced by many factors with the most imperative being the story of the artist and represented values. All the other functions should abide by this as accessories to confirm the artist's story and spread the concept as far as possible. When these business components are played accordingly, management has correctly branded an artist. Constant monitoring will avert disasters from distractions along the way.

Resources vary over time, requiring plans and implementation to assess economic impacts and potential contribution. This requires goals being divided into series and prioritization of optimal paths to the end game through short term goal acquisition. Each action and operation has by extension its own anticipation measures, sometimes planned and other times unexpected.

Never underestimate the power of experience in anticipation management. Don't strive for success at any cost, instead be reasonable. Measure the success of different operations and consider whether repeating the same patterns is useful. Remember that anticipation is also about the reactions of others, not just your own resources.

In any case, increase your experience whenever possible.

A manager can also operate on the sidelines and not all actions need to be related to the artist. It's not a bad idea to test something new, even in daily industry interactions. If the idea resonates and, most importantly, you get firsthand information about how it's received, you can incorporate it into the artist's activities. Keep in mind, a manager also possesses their own online presence that can be utilized for various outputs, both visible and invisible. Through experience, one also learns to better utilize the features of passive promotion to complement active promotional efforts.

Additionally, the better the industry associates the manager with the artist, the better the manager's influence can be significant for the artist's promotion as an independent factor.

7.3. Reactions

Every time an artist undertakes an action they must try in advance to assess the potential reactions of their audiences. At the beginning of your career, you do not usually have the experience required to make these assessments, awareness grows through practice. We can however make some assumptions based on the audiences, which tend to have different preferences. Fans and followers expect new music, merchandise, live venues and other artist-related products such as NFT's. It is of essence that everything progresses naturally and allows time for appreciation of new actions. In terms of the modern music business, you should always have your next single or step ready to go. Make sure it is in line with the story so far to avoid discrepancies, especially if your career is new. Living for the story is the major goal. With anticipation, we try to ensure the most important features receive the reaction they deserve.

This can be complex if audience expectation is far from what the artist wants them to feel. Take this into account but remember to move gradually at a pace appropriate for the audiences. Like previously said, we are almost constantly dealing with various preconditions – things without which a certain main goal cannot be achieved. If we need to implement a strategic deviation somewhere – be it with the audience and their expectations, or for the algorithms to understand our message correctly, it must be done. The way we handle these obligations can be unique. Remember that different methods can lead to the same goals. To that end, it is important to find your own style.

As they say, sometimes you have to think of this as a soap opera. During those quiet moments when it feels like your career isn't gaining momentum or the action has come to a halt, try to come up with something that moves the story forward. It doesn't have to be much, as long as it generates some movement.

Sometimes an expectation is for an artist to meet certain criteria. Perhaps the media won't take you seriously until you have a certain amount of followers on Instagram. If you want an interview, you should take action. A word of caution though as maximizing popularity shouldn't be the only goal and to be gained at any price. If an artist tries desperate measures to increase their popularity, it might not bode well for their credibility. These are delicate matters. A better approach is to present the same thing in a different light. If popularity isn't on your side, try another alternative method to showcase your point. You can always politely justify things because of your fans as everyone understands how important they are to an artist. What is of essence is to not blindly follow an audience's expectations beyond your own values.

For the industry this anticipation appears against their expectations. If you want the industry to take you seriously, you should act accordingly so they'll take note of your actions and react, reflecting in the content the media releases about you.

Industry operates with many unwritten rules. The more involved you are in the field, the better you start to understand them. By acknowledging these rules, you demonstrate your style and finesse and this alone may be a reason for your successes – at least in some respects.

Additionally, you can investigate your next contact through their social media, for example. Their last ten posts or reactions can reveal a lot about a person. This way, you can get some idea of who you'll be dealing with. Then you can compare this impression to what happens in a live situation. A manager's work involves a lot of personal observations as well.

You can learn from Google and search engines daily. If you are using your own website as a command center and monitoring results of what works and what doesn't, you are well positioned to to influence your active promotion through your own online presence. When you echo those themes across other social media platforms and also in physical encounters, you create understandable communication. Communication that different audiences in various contexts find easy to internalize.

As each stage towards a goal is considered and planned, so too should anticipation. The reactions of others are variables that you cannot completely control and may emerge at the same time. This is why it is important to understand motives.

Remember, motives vary. Some are personal, some are corporate goals – in addition, there are expectations, which differ across media, an audience and the industry. Whatever your goal may be, these variables should be considered when pursuing them.

Audiences may be disappointed in not receiving what they expected of an artist and the result can be a lacklustre reaction. It is good to realize that it isn't always because of a song. Perhaps a vital ingredient is missing like that of an artist being popular due to their care in what's happening around them, without which loses an audience's motivation to follow them. Being able to read these true motives and take them into account will make your job easier. Paying attention to super fans that spread information about you by their own initiative will give your story another important feature – interactivity. Failing to consider motives for other audiences and areas of action will let you down. It is your job to identify the motives.

At this point, it's essential to recall the storytelling style of soap operas. These shows run for decades and are created with the idea that new viewers are constantly coming in. As a result, the same series is followed by people with a solid understanding of the show's history, but also those for whom the stage is entirely new. This requires certain considerations for the narrative. It must provide something new for long-term viewers but remain straightforward enough for new viewers to grasp the plot quickly. The same applies to artists. This is why an organic run is what most artists aspire to. With natural storytelling that progresses seamlessly while also considering history and reasonable audience expectations, an artist can find themselves in a winning promotion scenario.

7.4. Motives

We have already touched on motives in this book, but now we will deal with them from the point of view of anticipation. Assuming the operation at hand is focused on a single mission the artist needs to take and the contribution of others. An operation may require certain reactions and/or acceptance from a recipient in order to be completed. The recipient may not be interested, but it is our job to convince them. However, remember to be polite and tactful and don't come on too strong. Try to gauge the situation correctly and do your homework well. You wouldn't want to later realize that the person you've been trying to persuade is already inherently against the idea. When considering personal motives and risk assessment, someone who has been in the industry and had a successful career to date may be more willing to take risks and better able to endure failure than someone new to the post. Or it could be the other way around. An operation may meet the personal needs of an individual looking for a promotion and thus they have additional motivation to move a project towards success. Overall feasibility is key to achieving success for an operation and needs to apply to everyone involved.

7.5. Self-Initiating Inclusions

Sometimes you insert ideas or hints without expecting an immediate effect. This could be described as the soap opera narrative. Its purpose is to sustain interest and generate the necessary movement. This narrative might not have explicit business objectives, but rather aims for communication with different audiences. However, this narrative framework can accommodate almost anything. An artist may have a dream or some valuable thing – possibly not even related to music. The original motive may not be revealed. There can be many reasons why this can be beneficial.

Recall the concept of episodes and story enrichment – events or a series of events that happen around an artist. They may happen without effort, from your own activity, but also as a reaction of others. We must decide what to do with them. Sometimes economic results are aimed for and sometimes we use them to facilitate passive promotion. Story enrichment is always intentional and self-initiating. Episodes are always about things that have already happened, whereas story enrichment applies to things that have not yet happened. This is somewhat artificial as we have no way other than through hope that the inclusions will turn into something.

This is indeed an interesting and challenging interface. Especially if everything is going well and progressing organically, how much more is needed, or even needed at all? Artists often face the need for change for various reasons and the need to develop something new. Many times, these new elements can be classified as artificial – they haven't materialized yet. Secondly, they come with an expectation of popularity, whether from the artist themselves, the industry, or the media. Therefore, in all additions, you always have to think about how to react if the end result doesn't meet expectations.

Consider an artist wanting to perform at a well-known venue – Wembley for example. Whilst their popularity isn't sufficient to even dream about this (yet) it is decided to include in their story line. The artist may decide to write a song about it – Live at Wembley. The lyrics contain metaphors – what it means and why. The metadata within the song connects to the digital realm and starts to have a life of its own. No success claims need to be made. Interest and an online history will be built around the song each time it's played – to fans, industry and the media. It may be that this song alone triggers the events that eventually lead to an appearance at Wembley. Information is disseminated beyond your sphere of influence and you don't have to do anything to maintain the idea. The setting is made for the future. If a show at Wembley occurs, you would likely be included in the event's marketing. This solidifies the affiliation.

Consistency takes place in the details so be careful. You do not want to cause any distractions for any audiences when your story progresses towards its goal. These self-initiating inclusions do not initially involve other audiences, only Google and the rest of the digital realm, so you do not necessarily need to concern other audiences. But you need to ensure search engines understand your message correctly. Then it's just follow-up. If audiences 'swallow the feed', their reactions may enable your dream. Audience reactions and interactions lay a foundation for the story-on-story effect. A version that might end up in a place where a Wembley booking is planned.

Self-initiating inclusions can be used for anything, even revealing an artist's interests. Inclusions should happen when appropriate, never as an artificial attempt to make an impact. When done correctly, the story comes alive. People get excited about things that excite you, providing a certain power and drawing attention.

A word of caution to not use these things just to get reactions. You have to mean it. The content must be real. This is a manifestation of the power of social media. Commenting on a social media conversation chain, you should prepare to spend two days with it. It may easily gather reactions, even lead to a completely different destination. That's why it is so important to be honest and not create false impressions. Some good advice is to proceed step by step – especially if you need others' contributions to succeed, presenting everything at once might be overwhelming. Allow the situation time to settle, especially when dealing with new things. The more confident you become, the more you know what to do with it. Remember everything leaves a mark.

Passive ideas are not just for fans, but also other audiences. Background concepts enhance the probability of being understood and connecting with your fans and other audiences. Consider when you look back as a 70 year old, will you be satisfied with everything said and written about you? Don't do things just because others are doing it. Be honest with yourself.

One potential future scenario also deserves attention. Imagine if accuracy becomes the most significant competitive advantage in the digital realm. Artists would be assessed based on whose online presence is the most accurate – even down to percentages – and this would influence how algorithms compare them with each other. Such a possibility, even if it never materializes, is a reason in itself to invest in an organic run.

8. BUSINESS

8.1. The Concept

The final piece of our deliberation and hence the destination, is the business. Everything mentioned above is a precondition for it. Facilitating preconditions alongside the story narrative establishes a foundation for business. If it's not yet clear, releasing music is the most essential part of the story narrative. That's the only way to establish the story root. Some business functions automatically – thanks to modern music business, while some requires active effort, monitoring, planning and execution. Sometimes the outcome is intentional while some business takes place coincidentally. That's the nature of the music business – you can succeed economically even without specifically trying to.

The nature of copyright enables one great option – freedom of choice. As copyright owner, the artist decides. If you allow a charity organization to use your music free of charge, you may do so. You control the use and terms.

This freedom of choice also allows you to perform a free function so that another product is sold. For example, issue free electronic pins with a link to the artist's website. The paid merchandise can then be found there.

On the other hand, if you want to do business in all music business forums, it can eat unnecessary resources – in the form of additional labor and unnecessary cooperation. The reasonable concern is how much it makes sense to increase business and related functions. From time to time it's only wise to ask yourself what is enough. The world of music business easily sucks you in, with all of its opportunities.

8.2. Starting Point

As we near the end, there is some repetition. While the topic is business, this section also marks the conclusion of this book. Therefore, if it seems that a paragraph starts the same way as before, its content may still be somewhat different – or offer a new perspective.

In terms of business and the related control, it is unwise to give up equities too early. As you sign away equities, you forfeit control – to some point. The following steps may not necessarily be in your hands anymore. Even though the world has changed, there still exists a notion in the industry that an artist needs industry approval before they can succeed in their career. This belief might prove costly if not countered with valid reasons. Without any added value or benefits from internal industry arrangements, it's not always advisable to agree to such terms. The matter can be complex because there might also be merits to internal industry arrangements.

As already pointed out, in some stages operations require external resources and third-party arrangements. In return we usually give up something. In the ideal situation this is balanced. External resources should only be used for the cause and when the need is exhausted, the original setting would return and the rights granted should return back to us. This relates not only to business control, but also artistic freedom.

From a business point of view the keyword is the cause, the reason why we ended up in such arrangements. Early on these arrangements are fairly standard. As business grows and wealth is acquired, we begin to have a choice. This is where our plan steps into the picture – the thing we are after. To get to the top requires infrastructure to support our music through the required attention, but if we intend to proceed organically as popularity allows, the situation is different. Everything is related to the resources we have and the plan. All new episodes and enrichments happen only if operations generate something. In this way we avoid external help until there's a reason for it.

Organic progress manifests in various dimensions. It implies progression that is carried out without intermediaries, adapting to situations and needs as people come into play. When the artist's story and promotional results guide the artist in a particular direction, their manager meets people as the process unfolds. This way, a valuable network grows, evolves and forms according to the significance each party brings to it. Every interaction provides new experiences and with this knowledge, new options for promotional tools and choices are obtained. At the same time, information about the artist and their activities circulates through channels recognized by others within the industry. This marks a significant difference from promotion carried out without such a tangible connection to the industry, but directed straight to the public.

The most sustainable way is to grow organically with no artificial operations. Each fan is your fan because they want to be. Active listeners are those including our songs on their personal playlists, here for the music or some other reason related to you. Each interview the result of something, not a premature statement of some unrealized issue. Your recording agreement came about because of your story and the music. Organic growth takes time and eats resources, so we may accelerate this process by artificial and premature means to avoid exhausting resources before acquiring the goal. This is the first stage to consider the process economically – as a business and for a business to succeed you need to be organized. Typically, promotion progresses by utilizing both organic and artificial means. The artist's management regulates them based on what the current situation demands.

8.3. Organization

The optimal artist organization is light and agile, adapting quickly to conditions. The more complex and consuming, the more difficult to react. The more diverse motivational circles form within an artist's organization, the harder it becomes to manage. Such expansion may occur entirely unnoticed. If an artist's activities seem appealing, it naturally attracts attention. When everyone wants to contribute, it tends to introduce elements that are unrelated to the artist's narrative. Allowing this to happen or further developing business around these elements poses the risk of leading the artist's career in the wrong direction. The starting point is that each participant should have a clear function – a role within the whole. In this way, their contribution is justified.

To decide what is fair you can evaluate contributions by imagining where you would be without it. This can be difficult to define precisely and you may find it more useful to use industrial norms such as manager agreements lasting two years, entitling the manager to two years post-termination compensation. Recording agreements with a label usually result in ownership of master recordings, either wholly or partially. The more options granted for the future for unrealized things, the weaker your position. Circumstances change. You don't want to be locked into something, and thereby, to exclude future possibilities that you're not yet aware of. A year can be a relatively long time in the music business. Working with humans can lead to things happening for no apparent reason. Agreements should allow for an exit and always correspond to current states of affair and give you a chance to react accordingly. So, when you build an organization, always consider whether copyright is always the reason to keep it together. Can you get people committed through means other than granting rights to the most valuable property?

8.4. Passive Income

Because of these variables, it is imperative to get passive income to a level sufficient for living and career moves, where the majority of revenue comes from automatic sources such as streaming payouts and composition royalties. As a business goal, this is the highest achievable level. Annual progress can show how close or far you are from that milestone. This is a reason to continually produce new material. The more music, the more amassed revenue or likelihood for a hit.

If agreements and/or arrangements are done well, you no longer have to work for them. With constant demand, you automatically receive annual settlements. A reminder however that copyright in itself does not require registration, but royalties and other copyright payouts are difficult without, which is why split sheets clarify ownership of songs for submission to copyright organization administrations. Ensure split sheets for recordings are done correctly before uploading music to digital streaming providers such as Spotify, Apple Music, Amazon Music etc. When these stages are completed, your position is clear and your passive income set up.

You should be affiliated with a Performance Rights Organization (PRO) that has reciprocal arrangements with a global collective management network, resulting in the PRO being able to collect your performance royalties worldwide. An artist may need to join more than one PRO if there are geographical differences to cover the world. That is, ensure that your PRO is indeed collecting royalties from all the countries where you are active.

You must also ensure the song specifics are correctly provided to avoid discrepancies and issues with payouts. Mechanical royalties may be a trickier case to handle as in some countries, you are not entitled to mechanical royalties unless you are a publisher or through a music publishing agreement with a real music publisher. This is where Songtrust and related collective management organizations step in. Affiliation enables mechanical royalties. This is important because streaming is classified for both performance and mechanical royalties. To fully access them, you should have collective representation in both. These collective management organizations usually allow you to determine the period of time they are in charge of your song. Check as conditions may change over time. For example, at the time of writing this book, through CD Baby, it's possible to manage mechanical royalties concurrently. Such arrangements might become more common in the future. You may have an alternative way to handle collective management of your compositions while uploading your recordings to streaming services. If you end up with a music publisher agreement later on, you may terminate this agreement and let the publisher handle the rest.

Songtrust also has publisher clients to assist small-businesses with the laborious tasks and obligations involved in setting up mechanical royalty collection. You should check these things prior to signing any agreement as it is important to rule out organizational chains that may weaken positions and shares.

The same principles apply with recordings. Ensure your contribution is correctly recorded to enable passive income. To get performance royalties from recordings, you need to join respective copyright organizations, like PPL in UK. Radio play of phonograms is not covered by performance royalties in all countries, in some it only applies to the composition. The world changes constantly concerning copyrights and related payments though, so it is smart to check this.

Direct streaming payouts from digital service providers must also be settled. Each artist decides how these payments are divided to each member. A recording agreement usually determines revenue division between the artist and the label. If you are independent, you will need to proceed through digital aggregators, or distributors, such as DistroKid, Tunecore, Symphonic Distribution, Corite or United Masters.

Manager passive income shares are derivative and determines in conditions of the management agreement.

8.5. Promotion

When all this is in place, it is time to start creating demand or attraction for the work through promotion. From a business point of view, action should be focused where performance is best.

It is important to understand the kind of promotion. To gain copyright economic value and hence passive income, you must support that mission. When we start discussing business, we need to think broadly. Today's music business may not be limited to operating solely within the realms specific to music. There's nothing stopping us from thinking outside the box or leveraging the clout we've gained elsewhere. An artist doesn't always differ from influencers. It's entirely possible that, propelled by your online presence and its associated significance, you'll generate revenue from the most unexpected places. The crucial aspect in all of these is alignment – how it fits into your story. Whether an artist is popular through other means than their music or live venue shows sell out instantaneously must be taken into account before executing any plan. If business occurs mainly through live performances, you should probably focus on that. This comes down to choices and resources, although some measures require more effort than others. What is the probability of success and time and resources required, and how does this relate to our current plan? Don't put all your eggs in one basket.

New business opportunities emerge in the music industry all the time, often thanks to new technologies or other arrangements. You should consider your knowledge in these areas as well as the additional acquisition of partners in such an endeavour. It is not necessarily as straight forward as it seems and make take considerable time to set up, compromising other areas of operation, with payout only happening six months down the line. Every time you step into a new business territory, it's a conscious risk. In the music business, especially concerning revenue forms related to copyrights, payments may have a delay. The larger the project, the more crucial it is to have reserves. It's not a bad idea to set aside a portion of your income – you never know when you'll encounter a business opportunity you can't overlook.

The situation might also be complicated by overlapping initiatives. It's the management's task to regulate these as the projects progress and to change course if necessary.

In an example of the complexity of promotion and its interdependence on the online presence, the generation of NFT's may not just be to make a profit, but also expand the age range of the target audience. Going viral on TikTok or some related platform may also achieve this. Anything is possible here and not everything is as it seems at face value.

All things have a lifetime however, and the main rule is when something ends, you should create something new. It is important to monitor progress also from the story point of view, not just business. Something still making a profit may no longer have impact and in order to proceed with promotion, you should add another chapter. Some things remain attractive and are still relevant without any promotion efforts.

There are many ways to deal with promotion – business is always popping up from a story in one way or another. How we enrich it dictates its topicality and attractiveness. In an ideal situation, the story has a life of its own and the audiences have their own perception of who you are and how they relate to your music. If public perception falls in line with your goal, promotion in terms of the story has succeeded. When this translates into economic results promotion has also succeeded in terms of business.

The question we need to ask from ourselves is what is enough. When are you satisfied? How are current and future efforts incorporated into existing operations?

This naturally depends on the stage of one's career. In the early stages, one has to seek financial significance for their story, production and themselves. Whenever such an opportunity arises, it's worth seizing. As an artist's career and financial stability gradually settle, there's more room for choice. You don't have to agree to everything anymore – from a purely business standpoint. In today's business landscape, not just in music, imagination is the only limit. The digital realm continually generates new methods to monetize various activities. Increasingly, these income-generating methods are automated. That is, you need to connect yourself to a mechanism and its digital recognition activates payments for your actions. Whenever something happens through your involvement, it triggers a payout accordingly.

One way to successfully embed inclusions in our operations may happen through publicity rights. The presence of the artist themselves without the 'official' connection to their music and related story. This, especially when popular, can be a market place in itself and lead to such things as granting use of their name, image and/or likeness to a commercial co-operation. This shouldn't burden other operations and requires a separate agreement outside official operations. It is important how much extra effort such an activity would take – if it is too much, it shouldn't be done.

Even though alternative ways to make business can be enormous opportunities, they may have their pitfalls. Always be cautious. Management should ensure there are back doors with appropriate waivers available for potential failures. The more popular you are, the more business proposals and it is crucial to evaluate the meaningfulness of each. Easy money and convenience may be against many risks, including your reputation. Make sure you cross all your t's and dot all your i's before taking on anything. If you cannot control something, you shouldn't invest too much in it. Consider your fans and the pros and cons of any action.

Even though this book discusses many modern approaches, traditional methods still have their place, especially in business. Through successful negotiations, you can secure an artist a sync placement, a record deal, or any other collaborative agreement that not only boosts their career, but also their finances. Managers are constantly scouting, searching and preparing for these kinds of situations. Any existing storyline or external factor can serve as a trigger for exploring such opportunities.

8.6. A Few Words About Modern Ideals

Modern ideals embrace having followers. The more, the better. Follower acquisition is one of the most important tasks – your own audience where you can tell your story without gatekeepers. Instant notifications as new content is uploaded or posted. Other audiences – industry, the media, the digital realm – can track this. Followers can introduce ideas or have a better description of something than your own version, which in turn can be used to your own advantage. Authentic interaction is the primary aim. It is one factor that makes an artist's online presence dynamic and vibrant.

Google also observes traffic around your actions to gain third-party notifications. This may increase the value of things referred to through multiple channels and be utilized further. Strengthening important content and not reacting to meaningless one, you also inform Google of its relevance. Google can then process this information and weigh its value.

At this point, it's good to think outside the box and explore things. You might come up with something entirely unique and fitting just for you. These are invaluable, especially when they happen in the digital realm. You might not even realize that you've invented something. Let's say an algorithm, in its classification, compares your music to ten similar artists. They all have the same typical way of promoting within that genre. However, in your case, there's a deviation in some key aspect. You've included a feature that others lack or do something differently. Somehow, this particular variable holds significant weight in how the algorithm supports your endeavors and their associated significance. When we talk about standing out increasingly in the digital sphere, this is what we mean.

It is not rare for artists to use paid promotion and other extra efforts for a momentary boost towards a certain goal. Paid promotion isn't always strictly for earning purposes, but also follower acquisition or other reasons. Extra efforts may be topical, for example trying to convince audiences to see things the way you want. Sometimes an artist feels that a Behind the Scenes is needed, but this may not be the marketing target.

In an ideal situation, your online presence and its associated passive promotion support all your current and future activities in the background. This combination, coupled with your personality, is what sets you apart from others.

Furthermore, just as the accuracy of information about yourself can be a significant promotional advantage, consistency can be as well.

It's typical that within a single task, multiple objectives are at play. Just like PR's secondary purpose is to improve an artist's online presence through optimization and SEO, within NFTs, there might be a secondary business aspect. Getting into blockchain, issuance of NFT's, or entering metaverses isn't just a modern fad, it allows a new type of ownership concept and many other business opportunities. For example, an artist can fund a particular production using crowdfunding instead of a record deal.

An artist also can own and administrate copyright together with their fans. As with all other features, you start with a single inclusion – and gain experience. Find out by experimenting. A song you don't plan on releasing to streaming services – perhaps NFT can find another use for it. Release it as an NFT with 20 percent ownership for buyers. Every time the NFT buyer sells it forward, the artist receives a piece as royalty, thus every transaction benefits both parties and gives the buyer a reason to trade. An NFT is therefore not necessarily a mere collectible, it may also establish ownership for the underlying copyright. Determine on a case-by-case basis conditions of issue. The above is just one example to make use of Web3 and its opportunities, with the NFT a joint interest for the artist and their fans.

The metaverse allows you to make more diverse modes within your operations. It is very likely you have to position yourself into its communities. How much resources are worth reserving depends on your action plan and the financial results sought. When we discuss an artist's story and its consistency, we encounter modern ideals. When an artist's narrative can generate meanings in an understandable, logical and credible manner, it enables these secondary business strategies. In the realm of modern ideals, these secondary methods might actually be the most effective, as their success and emergence often stem from the commitment of loyal fans.

An artist will probably utilize a combination of traditional and new business for which management's task is to allocate resources not only to business operations, but also the artist's story.

I am consciously careful with this matter. Development takes place quickly. The examples above may already be old when this book is published. Fortunately, this doesn't change the concept of music business management – new ways to tell the story, interact with fans and make business. How these opportunities are utilized depends entirely on the artist. It is likely Web3 becomes a viable function alongside traditional business making models. The future will show how artificial intelligence reshape this business. Remember that the most important thing for you is to incorporate these innovations into your operations at a pace that works best for you.

Nevertheless, one thing remains constant. It's consistency. Consistency makes actions credible and purposeful. In today's world where everything can be tracked, inconsistency is something that affects and is noticeable from afar.

It only takes a few seconds to see that things are not in order. Therefore, not just the online presence but the underlying operations should progress logically from one aspect to another.

Consider how new functions fit with the previous. Things can be adapted to fit in with background motives, but ensure at what cost. Don't become careless amid these opportunities. Even if new technology with its new features may appear as a fast-paced money machine, they might not have a place at the moment. Consider carefully these implementation situations, their coherence within the whole and when is the right time to adopt something new.

In this assessment, you can leverage the management compartments presented in this book, as well as the concept of the four audiences.

8.7. Fan Engagement and Acquisition

Another thing that cannot be forgotten amidst development is the fans. One of the most important goals in terms of business is to acquire fans – not just any fans, but active ones, sometimes referred to as super fans. For many artists, these fans are the whole engine, the more we have, the more noise they cause. There's a saying that fans cannot be wrong – if you have a million active fans, there must be a reason for it. Critics may say otherwise, but you have done something right. A wise man said it isn't always about artistic high standards, but the emotion it ignites.

The best case scenario will be fans find you through your music. Each new release results in activity that you don't need to do anything for. This is one of the main goals for business and results in generation of copyright-related revenue and passive income. Our job is to make this happen as naturally as possible.

There are many ways to start this journey, but it also depends what we are aiming for. If your goal is to be authentic, all engagements must be real from the start. All promotion is focused on where we can find true fans because they want to be. This is serious business and may require a hundred live performances a year to make it happen. If each venue acquires twenty fans, there's 2000 fans by the end of that year. Most are probably active and we can interact with them daily. Consider the advertising potential if each would talk to ten of their friends and they in turn become fans. Gigs may no longer be necessary to achieve your goals.

With one thousand fans subscribed to your Youtube channel you exceed the threshold to monetize your channel. This is completely different to 10 000 followers incited to follow you through ads, paid promotion or other artificial means. Real is always real. Of 10 000 followers, only 200 may become subscribers to your Youtube channel and do not necessarily have the same connection to you than organic connections created with people who have 'met' you in person and seen you live.

Followers do not always refer to fans. There's still work to do and it is now up to us to convince them we are worthy of their fandom. In doing so, avoid excessive compliance with industry generated ideals. Fan acquisition methods and advertising may not necessarily be for everyone. It is important to find your own style to handle this, which develops over time.

As mentioned, some artists primarily invest their efforts in passive promotion and its impact, with active promotion occurring primarily when necessary. When an artist builds a sufficient fan base, maintaining that connection is likely the most crucial operation. If a good atmosphere is cultivated there, the activity within that environment itself generates not only more fans, but also a unique culture of operation. Word of mouth remains an effective way to spread a message.

You then guide that impression on your online presence with different emphases at different times, resulting in the desired movement. When supported by active promotion, it creates an impact on the artist's narrative that resonates with fans and other audiences.

It isn't always a requirement that all your followers are active. Sometimes it's the amount that matters. You may be known for only one song and it is that song that people recognize you through. Later songs have no similar success, but your social media is highly active. You may be considered an artist, but following happens through other operations. Life in and of itself is the most interesting thing. A modern artist doesn't always differ much from influencers. Titles are irrelevant.

Without generating meaningful streaming revenue or other income typical to the music business, our business can still be relevant elsewhere and may not even require a story. It depends what your business goal is.

Fan engagement can be implemented in many ways and for many reasons. Be inventive. Competitions to win spare or excess merchandise or products can bring in subscriptions and followers. Then follow up to get better connected and continue to engage with them.

When it comes to merchandise, one crucial aspect to consider now and in the future is its environmental impact. It can significantly affect the types of merchandise produced for an artist. Therefore, ensure that your merchandise lineup and overall operations align with the values you stand for. Here, it's also essential to consider your fans' preferences. If environmental actions are important to them, it's a good idea to operate in alignment with these values from that perspective as well.

As a result some participants may end up fans for life – also for the music. This can be shared with friends, expanding your reach to their own sphere of influence both online and in person. Your effort, creates effort. Even if not strictly related to your music, it can be a game changer to your overall promotion, drawing attention to your activities, also in the future.

Social media influencers may take one of your songs and give it new meaning, resulting in social media following. It's not uncommon for an old song to get reheated in this way either. Connecting with influencers or sharing merchandise with them can further your online reach and add to your passive promotion.

Even though it is important to actively walk towards your target, it is similarly important to monitor what you have left behind. Play your 'Pokemon Go' right! If you succeed, you acquire another fan. As much as it is about creating meaning, it is also about people finding you.

8.8. Credits

It is extremely important for everyone to be appreciated in a way their contribution deserves. Credits are usually associated with the moral rights of copyright, the right to attribution and the right to integrity. There's economic meaning, but the indirect effects of such an inclusion may be even more valuable than the money, so it's important to also look at long-term effects.

CV (curriculum vitae) isn't necessarily a relevant instrument in the music business, unless you're working behind the scenes and need to prove your experience. You may be hired for a job because of a specific craft or a working method makes you an asset. What makes you valuable? Your contribution may also be used in music & tech innovations. Even if your work takes place behind closed doors, results may be visible and this is what's valuable within the industry. When appropriately credited your future opportunities are also increased.

LinkedIn is a platform where industry insiders communicate about credits. Before you start posting there, it's a good idea to observe how other industry players communicate. By following their lead, you'll find your own style and gradually begin to attract attention. If you're involved in a significant event, situation, production, or anything else related to the industry, request to mention it and share it on LinkedIn. Oftentimes, captions for these posts are planned together before, during and after such milestones. In any case, the more you showcase yourself through your own posts or by being tagged in these events, the wider your involvement will be noticed. LinkedIn is also a platform that is often checked when people want to find more information about you. If your online presence there is in good shape and supports your goals, it can be a significant asset for you in the future.

Even though industry approval is not as much of a barrier as it used to be, it still holds significance from this perspective – not necessarily approval, but awareness. When the industry becomes aware that you exist and that you exist in the role you desire, it furthers your endeavors. Today, the operations of the industry appear quite transparent, including your contribution within it. When you emerge in favorable contexts, it enhances your credibility – even in the eyes of those who haven't met you yet.

For artists, their production is a reference. Artists are responsible for the music they perform, record and write – to themselves or others and they receive credit for a new song, recording or other production. These credits are important to their progress in many respects. First of all, each credit establishes a permanent link to the production. Second, each credit has a defining role. When you release a song, you start being seen as an artist. A song can have multiple recordings and thus every time a new version is recorded and released, you are attached to it – if you have written or co-written it.

An ISWC code (International Standard Musical Work Code) links your participation with a song and gathers traffic every time it is performed. You may have more hits on your production than you as a person – another one good reason to ensure all the credits are written correctly.

An ISRC code (International Strandard Recording Code) is the same for recordings.

Credits may also have economic value per se. Your leverage is based on these credits and related success. Even if you are not popular at that precise moment, you may still use this foundation for future efforts. This connection can make an operation more impressive than without – from a search engine point of view. A new brand may use a connection as a foundation for future purposes and get a jumpstart, momentarily reaching first-page position of search results. If they get attached to it somehow. It is then up to the advertiser how to make use of this plug-in for their own endeavors.

In the future, having a strong background and substantial clout in a particular matter can be a reason in itself to secure an advertising deal. Especially if your actions and production hold significant weight within a particular theme. Advertisers may benefit greatly from the authenticity and relevance associated with it.

Commercials are different from movies and television series. A movie requires the permanent connection between its music and moving picture, whereas a commercial doesn't, therefore typically commercial advertisers only get music use for a limited period of time. Another commercial or reuse of the same commercial, may require an additional license. Indeed, similar license renewals also occur in the realm of movies and TV series. Of course the negotiation can go both ways. Connecting an artist and their music to commercials can attract better attention and including the artist's production metadata and publicity rights will increase the reach and meaning behind a collaboration.

For an artist credit inclusion is a remarkable opportunity. Whether by film or commercials, being included in the metadata and related credits of something that may become a blockbuster or associated with an advertiser like New Balance or Merrell, will increase awareness and likely economic rewards. It isn't merely about moral rights that makes credit important.

8.9. Meanings

As a conclusion, it is important to differentiate between story-related and business meanings – although they are often interdependent. We don't necessarily have to create business meaning – the story may do that automatically. How do we want to use the story for our goals? How much active input and output? We cannot always affect reactions. Public opinion and other audiences' reactions are the other side of the coin. When goals and reactions are in balance, we are good. Combining these provides an artist's overall image, which varies throughout a career.

When discussing the importance of standing out from others and how this differentiation increasingly occurs digitally, a small clarification is in order. This deviation doesn't have to be substantial; it simply needs to be sufficient and meaningful. More often than not, you'll naturally discover that deviation. Whenever something has to be forced, the end result can easily come across as contrived. Therefore, let things brew when you're not exactly sure what or how to do it.

Interference with the internal logic of a story, should be corrected. Lacking content, or losing power, requires additional efforts, which can be done in different ways as pointed out in this book. Explanations may be needed. Sometimes we create these interfering elements ourselves to increase resources, which requires design. Adjustments may be needed if audience reactions are not as expected to ensure overall image isn't compromised. As a main rule, before your digital identity is carved in stone in the eyes of all audiences, progress must be monitored constantly. After this, things become more flexible. Reaching this point is individual with some artists getting there before others.

Embracing consistency usually allows a seamless connection between the meaning of our goals and economic meaning, thus not requiring specific enrichments. This is what we strive for. Even if only for business reasons, there is still a story and its origin. The story also protects us when for example an artist's popularity wanes. Then you can steer attention to other important meanings. It is important to be aware of inert flaws in our operations. There can be long-term consequences of fans unhappy with something we have done, who don't specifically bring it up, but remain silent. Consider and anticipate the potential reactions of others.

Hidden meanings also need to be looked out for. You may not even know you are close to being offered a recording agreement or some other significant collaboration. You have appeared on a label's radar, which sometimes have the patience of a spider and don't necessarily inform you of their interest.

A manager's job is to evaluate and anticipate daily agendas from a short-term point of view and also map out long-term consequences. Getting short-term plans to work in favor of long-term plans is extremely important. Prioritize meanings. Lay out preconditions to fit into ongoing operations and ensure everything fits with the story. Natural developments may allow for a change in this and thus the meanings behind different operations. Ensuring seamless blending of these will safeguard the artist's overall image.

Money is meaningful – it impacts so many parts of an artist's overall operation. How much profit everyone gets, life situations – all impact decision-making. Give thought to the end. Apply the same kind of anticipation to your career as to your personal life.

Finally, the ideal setting sees your background in order. All essentials are self-perpetuating and you may freely include new activities just because it's fun. You are within the cumulative impact sphere of passive promotion. It positively responds to all movements related to the artist, management and operations. Further effort is unnecessary unless you want. People around you have a steady position and good memories, not just in terms of income, but are also credited in the way they deserve.

9. OUTRO

Naturally, there's more to music business management than the content of this book. I hope this book does justice to your endeavors and will assist you in facilitating them further. Make your own conclusions. Consider it as dinner served – only after you know how it tastes. My insights to add to yours. Your job is to make it better. If that happens, I have succeeded.

Whatever you do in the future, keep your vision clear. In the foreground, on that transparent wall, you see the three compartments of management. Behind them, you can see the four music business audiences, the areas of action. When you observe this business from this perspective, you'll stay on track even in challenging situations.

Technology can transform businesses, as well as enable new business models. As long as copyright exists, development doesn't fundamentally change anything. Your actions are guided by the operational plan you have in place at any given time in the face of all these possibilities. Trends come and go. You yourself determine how resources are allocated at any given time. You need to assess how far it makes sense to proceed on your own and where it's worth seeking support. For example, if a new feature of artificial intelligence introduces a business element, your first task is to examine it through the three compartments on that transparent wall and see the audiences and operational areas behind it. Next, you must decide what it means for you.

At this point I consider whether I have forgotten something, but whilst I follow my feelings, sometimes it is unwise to include additional details, especially in a non-fiction book. As time goes by, I may find other ways to add content, or a second edition.

And there you are, reading the second edition. Do you notice that in a non-fiction book, especially in music business management, it doesn't need to be all-encompassing? It's even better if it isn't. This way allows you to draw your own conclusions and even disagree with the content. In that case, the book serves its purpose beyond its contents.

This book is the first of its kind. In it I believe you get a comprehensive understanding of what the music business is in the 2020's. For me, this book will be a lasting foundation for the coming years and I will use this structure also in my lectures. To be honest, the content of this book has already been test-driven at Seinäjoki University of Applied Sciences. It's a great place to reflect on the content and have the interaction and see how students accept it.

So much so that a group of students from previous classes formed 'Manager Patrol' as we like to call it. When a sufficient number of students from various courses expressed their interest in this, we decided to create our own group. We meet weekly to discuss updates and take on tasks as we see fit. The underlying force behind all this, once again, is that much-talked-about organic run. This group has naturally evolved on its own.

When we add the artists I've used as examples in my lectures to the mix, we notice that a natural progression brought us here.

The best management is effortless and happens without force. If something feels good, it probably is good. Alternatively, if something doesn't feel right, it probably isn't. Of course, there will be moments of artificial effort or uncomfortable decisions. Remember you probably cannot have it all and this shouldn't be your goal. Trust me. The long run is more important so you can congratulate yourself when older. Play the long game. When you have done what feels best, you won't regret anything. It's been your path.

A wise manager learns the basics well – like you are doing now. The better you know the technical side of this business, the more you are aware of its possibilities, making you capable of using alternative strategies that will better serve everyone's needs. You will learn by doing and find your own style. Map out your strengths and steer them towards something meaningful. Personal development and engagement is the greatest obligation to yourself. With a sufficient amount of knowledge and experience, things will become easier. Then you can enjoy what you do. You may not always be able to control the situation, but you can control your mind. A good virtue for a manager to have. The world is in a state of confusion, but your mind is calm. You know the next sensible step. And that's often what your clients will be after – that you stand strong by their side.

Remember the artist is also a resource. Don't forcibly manage something if an artist can handle the matter better themselves. Be subtle with your own suggestions. In the wrong place at the wrong time, they may disrupt the artist's mental and artistic equilibrium. Your own enthusiasm may cloud the fact an artist does not necessarily want to do something. Also, each manager initiative should go through the artist, unless approval is already self-evident.

Like said at the beginning of this book, there are also other materials you should know. For example, Donald Passman's All You Need To Know About The Music Business is a great book to read. As is Artist Management for the Music Business by Paul Allen. Get accustomed and know the more regularly you deal with related information, the easier it becomes. Anticipate the content. This is what management is about. Control the space the best you can.

Don't presume you know how a manager should be. Not all managers are talkative, especially today. No one knows who will succeed. There's plenty of room – for all of us. Preparedness rules the world. Your window of opportunity may emerge from anywhere, even the most improbable of places. Be ready. The right factor isn't always the most obvious one. Never underestimate preparation, no matter how far away a goal seems to be. Forget distracting expectations, not all are good. Do not compare yourself to others. You do not know all the circumstances. Embrace yourself, what you have and only take assignments that make you feel good. But still make sure you have an exit! You do not want success at any cost.

Remember that music industry professionals often have a plan B, C and even D. Even when your current position seems secure, it's wise to have backup plans. When you receive funds from an operation, don't spend them right away. Save a portion. Learn this habit and it will serve you well in the future. You never know what opportunities the day might bring. If an invitation comes and you need funds, it won't be a barrier. You'll be able to travel to the event even at short notice.

Now, my Friend it is time to finish this book. I thank you for reading, it means a lot to me. If something continues to bother you or remains unclear – feel free to ask. E-mail me. My contact info is on my website – https://mikakarhumaa.fi. And yes, I do offer one-on-one appointments. If you need support with building your online presence or anything else related to music business management, feel free to schedule an appointment. You'd be surprised to know how many interactions I have with my readers.

BIBLIOGRAPHY

The Essence of the Music Business: Contracts, 2nd Edition (2019)
The Essence of the Music Business: Philosophy, 2nd Edition (2020)
The Essence of the Music Business: Strategy, 2nd Edition (2021)